0095818

D0353220

Training in the age of the learner

Martyn Sloman was appointed to his current position in 2001. Before joining the CIPD he was Director of Management Education and Training at Ernst & Young. Martyn is an Honorary Professor in the School of Management and Languages, Heriot Watt University, Edinburgh, an Honorary Teaching Fellow in the Department of Organisational Psychology at Birkbeck College, University of London and an Industrial fellow at Kingston Business School.

The Chartered Institute of Personnel and Development is the leading publisher of books and reports for personnel and training professionals, students, and for all those concerned with the effective management and development of people at work. For details of all our titles, please contact the Publishing Department:

tel: 020-8263 3387
fax: 020-8263 3850
e-mail: publish@cipd.co.uk
The catalogue of all CIPD titles can be viewed on the CIPD website:
www.cipd.co.uk/bookstore

Training in the Age of the Learner

Martyn Sloman

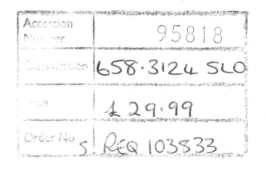
Chartered Institute of Personnel and Development

Design by Beacon GDT
Typesetting by Fakenham Photosetting Ltd, Fakenham, Norfolk
Printed in Great Britain by The Cromwell Press, Trowbridge, Wiltshire

British Library Cataloguing in Publication Data
A catalogue record for this book is available from the British Library

ISBN 0–85292–991 9

Dedication
To the memory of Bill Gregory,
National Organiser, Workers' Educational Association, 1948–1956
Extramural Department, University College, Cardiff, 1956–1970.

The Lord God has given me the tongue of a teacher,
that I may know how to sustain the weary with a word.
Isaiah 50:4

Chartered Institute of Personnel and Development, CIPD House,
Camp Road, London SW19 4UX
Tel: 020 8971 9000   Fax: 020 8263 3333
E-mail: cipd@cipd.co.uk Website: www.cipd.co.uk
Incorporated by Royal Charter. Registered Charity No. 1079797.

It is clear that there really is a new agenda emerging and it's about learning not training. This book sets out the evidence for the shift, explains the implications of it and has some great practical examples of how different organisations have been trying to make this shift. Anyone who is interested in the area will find this of real value.

Kevin Hogarth
Director of International Resourcing
Capital One Bank (Europe) plc

With his focus firmly on the learner, not the technology, Martyn Sloman is truly the spokesman of the eLearning revolution. And he writes with a style and panache quite unlike the typical dreary business tome. Read this book learn and be entertained at the same time!

Kenneth Fee
Chief Executive, The eLearning Alliance

This well timed book offers readers a thought provoking rationale for placing learning not just at the heart of the individual, but also of the organisation. Sloman demonstrates how learning is now imperative for change, competitive advantage and progress. Giving a thorough analysis of all the different factors this book provides a compelling argument and practical examples of how to radically transition training.

The results you will gain from this book will be a much deeper understanding of the whole process of learning, including blended. You will know how to deliver accelerated performance that really does make a difference, even to bottom line measures.

Sue Harley
Managing Director, IQdos Ltd

Contents

Acknowledgements

I express my appreciation to the following publishers and organisations for their permission to include extracts and quotations from published works.

Harvard Business Review for PORTER, M. (2001) 'Strategy and the Internet', Copyright © March 2001 the Harvard Business School Publishing Corporation. All rights reserved.

The International Labour Office for ASHTON, D. A. *and* SUNG, J. (2002) *Supporting Workplace Learning for High Performance Working*. Geneva, International Labour Office.

The American Society for Training and Development for PISKURICH, G. M. *and* SANDERS, E. S. (1998) *ASTD Models for Learning Technologies*: *Roles, Competencies and Outputs*. Human Performance Improvement Certificate Program. Also an extract from ROTHWELL, W. (2003) *ASTD Models for Human Performance Improvement*.

The Executor, Henry Reed Estate, for the extract from *Naming of Parts*.

Strategy & Business for TAPSCOTT, D. (2001) *Rethinking Strategy in a Networked World*. Issue 24, 3rd Quarter; pp.37–41.

Sun Microsystems for JAMES, C. *Enterprise Talent Management: Need, Opportunity and Challenges*.

Kogan Page for table adapted from p.220 of STEPHENSON, J. (ed) (2001) *Teaching and Learning Online*. London. Kogan Page.

Orion Books for NAUGHTON, J. (2001) *A Brief History of the Future*. London, Phoenix.

AMACOM (a division of the American Management Association, New York) for BOZZONE, V. (2002) *Speed to Market: Lean Manufacturing for Job Shops*. Reprinted by permission of the publisher from the second edition, Copyright © 2002 Vincent Bozzone. All rights reserved. http://www.amacom.books.org

Wadsworth for the Robert Gagne quote. From the *Conditions of Learning: Training applications*, 1st edn by GAGNE © 1996. Reprinted with permission of Wadsworth, a division of Thompson Learning: www.thompsonrights.com. Fax 800 730 2215.

Training Journal and *Human Resources Decisions International* for permission to reproduce material by the author that had previously appeared in their publications

... And to the Chartered Institute of Personnel and Development and *People Management* for the many extracts from books, research reports, change agendas and articles that appear throughout this book.

Preface

Three years ago I had the good fortune to be offered a position at the Chartered Institute of Personnel and Development (CIPD), which gave me the scope to develop my ideas on training and learning. The stimulus that led me to produce a book came from my colleagues. Throughout the period of its production all the CIPD advisers were generous in their support and encouragement. My thanks then to them, especially to Mike Cannell, Victoria Gill and Jessica Rolph who worked with me in the Learning, Training and Development Portfolio, and to Angela Baron, Mike Emmott and John Philpott. Special thanks also go to my bosses, Geoff Armstrong and Duncan Brown, who supported the project from the outset.

The following people assisted by reading drafts: Judith Cowan, Elizabeth Fisher, Peter Honey, Nickie Fonda, Ann Jakeman, Karen Jaques, Jake Reynolds and Michelle Selinger. All of them willingly found time to share their ideas. The publishers and organisations who generously granted permission to reproduce extracts and quotations are listed above. I am grateful to them and to many other people who allowed me to draw on their work; I have acknowledged them at appropriate points in the text. Many training managers took time out of their busy schedules to provide input from their organisations; without their contribution it would have been impossible to move beyond analysis and into the issues surrounding implementation.

Kim Andrews typed and organised the manuscript. This is the third time we have worked together on a book and I have become increasingly reliant on her patience and support. Thanks also to the staff of the CIPD Library and Information Services – most especially to Steve Corbett.

This book was written in Norfolk where my wife, Anne, has again supported and tolerated sustained weekend and holiday work. Her understanding has made the project possible. In this time of turbulence it is comforting to know that some things remain constant. In the Acknowledgements in my first training book, published in 1994, I expressed thanks to the Welsh Rugby team for playing so dismally that they scarcely offered a distraction. Nine years on I can repeat those thanks without amendment.

Finally, a word about the short cameos that have been inserted at the beginning of each chapter. During the early 1990s I headed a training function at a large investment bank. It was a period when a well-known recruitment consultant advertised a job in the following term: 'Unpleasant training manager – If you only really care about people and the fulfilment of human potential, perhaps you should be a missionary.' *The Economist* once described investment banks as 'among the worst-managed institutions on the planet because they are built on a loose confederation of franchises and outsize egos' (16 October 2002, p.90). All the cameos – bar one apocryphal story – describe real incidents that took place at the bank. Nevertheless we seemed to make a deal of headway when we bypassed the macho culture and worked with the learners.

It is amazing and encouraging how much has changed in a decade; how much more receptive the atmosphere towards training in organisations is today. The opportunity is there – all we have to do is deliver. If this book assists some readers to achieve their aims in their organisation, my efforts will have been worthwhile.

Martyn Sloman
Norfolk 2003

List of figures

List of tables

Introduction:
The age of the learner

The first decade of the 21st century offers a unique window of opportunity for those involved in delivering training and promoting learning in organisations. We can expect to work in a new way, which will be both more effective and more satisfying. Currently we are operating in a period of considerable turbulence. This can make the determination of short-term action difficult. In order to take advantage of this new opportunity we need to look beyond the short term and develop new approaches based on a new mindset.

This, it is contended, is the challenge faced by many of those involved in the provision of human resource development and training in organisations today. Such people may be directors or senior managers (in human resources or in general management positions), specialist trainers or developers, or consultants designing or delivering the training interventions on a contractual or outsourced basis. Increasingly they are aware that the assumptions that underpin their thinking are changing as these new opportunities are arising. The challenge is to understand the nature of the transition, produce clear guidelines, and translate them into actions which will assist the organisation in the achievement of its objectives.

The central argument of this book is that the best way forward is for trainers to adopt a new paradigm. The paradigm proposed is aspirational. It shifts the focus from training to learning. It reflects the dynamic and irresistible forces that will shape the environment in which training is delivered. It has the potential to create a win-win situation in which organisations, individual learners, and society as a whole will benefit. The paradigm is summarised immediately below. It will be referred to hereafter more simply as 'a focus on the learner' or 'learner-focus'.

Interventions and activities that are intended to improve knowledge and skills in organisations will increasingly focus on the learner. Emphasis will shift to the individual learner (or the team), and he or she will be encouraged to take more responsibility for his or her learning. Efforts will be made to develop a climate that supports effective and appropriate learning. Such interventions and activities will form part of an integrated approach to creating competitive advantage through people in the organisation.

It is hoped that the terminology used will not act as a deterrent or a barrier. In fact, as will be seen, much of what underlies this new approach is well understood. Training professionals will find themselves on familiar ground as the arguments are developed in this book. What is required is not the articulation and acquisition of a new set of skills and capabilities. What is required is a new mindset – a new way of looking at their world.

This requirement for a new mindset is why the word *paradigm* rather than *model* has been chosen to describe this focus on the learner. A paradigm can be viewed as a conceptual framework in which theories are constructed. The phrase 'paradigm shift' is used to describe the pervasive changes that can result from a new discovery, and which demand an entirely new perspective. They inevitably result in a change in the way in which we think and act (Kuhn, 1962[1]).

As has been noted, this new paradigm demands a shift from training to learning. An understanding of this distinction is fundamental to the arguments developed in this book; some definitions and illustrations may assist. The following is an extract from *How do People Learn?*, a research report commissioned by the Chartered Institute of Personnel and Development and written by Cambridge Programme for Industry (p.9).

> *Learning is the process by which a person constructs new knowledge, skills and capabilities, whereas training is one of several responses an organisation can undertake to promote learning.*[2]

In short, learning lies in the domain of the individual – people learn in all sorts of ways, whether by intention or accident. Training, however, is a deliberate act by the organisation; it is an intervention designed to achieve an organisational objective.

People learn bad things as well as good. Many people in organisations learn how to augment their expenses. They learn from others, or by trial and error, how far they can push the limits. This is learning. However, there is no training course available labelled 'Inflating your expenses – an introduction' or 'Inflating your expenses, the international Dimension (participants must have attended Inflating your expenses – an introduction before registering for this event)'. This light-hearted example illustrates how much learning that takes place in organisations is independent of training activities. We have, as trainers, known this for some time. We have spoken positively about informal learning and learning on-the-job. We have not, however, appreciated the powerful consequences that may follow from a recognition of this distinction.

In the first chapter of this book the forces that give rise to the new paradigm of learner-focus will be outlined. They will be identified as new perspectives on competitive advantage, which are inextricably linked with the new opportunities created by information technology. The second chapter of the book develops the case for the new paradigm by considering the traditional perspectives, or models, of training. It will be argued that these traditional models, which have underpinned much of our approach to knowledge and skills enhancement in the workplace, have concentrated on the role of the trainer rather than the process of learning. They are training, not learning models. This is not to denigrate their value, and most certainly not to denigrate their authors; it is simply that a new paradigm is required.

The third chapter, which completes the first Part of the book, will discuss how people learn at work. An appreciation of what we know about learning is a prerequisite to developing and implementing learner-focused approaches.

Much of the recent debates on learning and training in organisations has been concerned with the opportunities that have arisen as a result of new technology. E-learning and its adolescent offspring, blended learning, have become the latest hot topics. They will be considered in some depth in Chapters 4 and 5, which together form the second Part of this book. Crucially, it will be argued that the new technology of the Internet is best seen as a vital enabling mechanism. It will allow the focus on the learner to take place in a way that hitherto was not possible. Properly managed, it could allow aspirations to become reality.

This move through to implementation forms the third Part of the book. Chapter 6 reviews the role of the trainer and what is needed to make the new approaches work. Chapters 7 and 8 consider some detailed implementation issues. These chapters ask what interventions and activities are needed when we focus on the learner, as opposed to delivering training. The word *intervention* will appear frequently in the text and should be justified at the outset.

As will be argued in the final sections of the book, the key to success is embedding good learning practices into organisational activity. Appropriate and effective learning must become part of 'the ways things are done here'. Sometimes this will occur naturally and sometimes it will arise through the efforts of the learners themselves. However, in most organisations those responsible for training and learning spend their time undertaking a series of activities which can be seen as interventions designed to assist individuals acquire skills and knowledge or create a climate in which this becomes possible. The nature of the interventions will change as we shift our focus – this will be a continuing theme throughout the third Part of the book – but they will be interventions none the less. Resources, both time and money, will be expended to try and make things operate differently.

Before this Introduction is concluded, one other important feature of the new paradigm should be considered. This is the use of the term *aspirational*. As will be seen, many organisations are taking, and still more considering, activities that could be described as having a focus on the learner. However, the paradigm of learner-focus is put forward as an aim, not a statement of existing reality. It is something that we should strive towards creating, rather than a description of current best practice.

For this reason, the approach to case study illustrations has been to use examples of emerging good practice rather than identifying best practice organisations. The latter approach has, in any case, been one of the curses of the modern training and general management literature. Organisations and circumstances change – how many Enron case studies were under preparation in 2001? At this stage in the transition from training to learning it would be a very bold organisation that would claim to have identified all that needs to be done and be well on the way to doing it. Regrettably, the recent early stages of e-learning were bedevilled by over-promotion, particularly by vendors but also unfortunately by the specialist press and government, of case examples which proved to have little substance after examination. If we are to manage effectively wider challenges involved in the transition from training to learning, a more critical perspective will be required.

Most of the companies, public sector and voluntary sector bodies contacted during the period in which this book was produced responded tentatively. They recognised the importance of the issues, and were constructing their forward agenda, but were anxious not to be portrayed as exemplars for the world. In these circumstances their willingness to supply such information is especially helpful.

So, to summarise, 'learner-focus' is an aspirational paradigm which reflects modern business and economic reality; making it happen is today's challenge for the profession. The first chapter of the book considers the circumstances in which this opportunity has arisen.

REFERENCES AND READING

1 In 1962 Thomas Kuhn, the distinguished American scientist and academic, produced an important essay on scientific revolutions. He explored the importance of paradigms and their effect on the nature of scientific enquiry. KUHN, T. (1962) *The Structure of Scientific Revolutions*. Chicago, University of Chicago Press.
2 REYNOLDS, J., CALEY, L. and MASON, R. (2002) *How Do People Learn?* Research Report produced by Cambridge Programme for Industry for the CIPD.

Part 1

Creating the mindset

1

The new competitive advantage

In the late 1980s I left management consultancy to take up a job as Head of Training at a large investment bank. It was a tough environment. The City was full of self-confidence after Big Bang. However, HR practices often resembled the activities of a Wild West sheriff, with efforts to maintain law and order at the frontier, rather than long-term attempts to built organisational capability. I well remember my introductory meeting with one of the Heads of Business. No sooner had I ventured through the door when he told me his view was that the training function should be abolished. Put on the back foot, I informed him that a number of his staff had expressed interest in the company MBA that we were about to establish. His response was immediate. 'Give me their names and I'll sack them.'

Fifteen years have passed since the Business Head at the investment bank expressed his forthright views. In this time there has been a growing recognition of the importance of effective training and learning to the future of the business. 'People are our most important assets', or its variant, 'Our most important assets walk out of the door at night', has emerged as one of the more popular management aphorisms of our time. True, much of what has passed has been rhetoric rather than reality. For the 1990s it would be difficult to point to enduring changes which would indicate a sustained commitment from employers to invest in the knowledge and skills of staff. Good practice certainly existed in some sectors: many organisations committed to the government-supported 'Investors in People' standard.[1] However, if there has been a systematic increase in learning and training, it did not show up in any published statistics. Moreover, a perceived lack of investment in training by employers has remained a constant area of concern for government for at least two decades.

As we enter the first decade of the 21st century there is every possibility, and some indications, that significant changes are taking place. New business forces will lead to greater emphasis on training and learning, and a shift from the former to the latter. The argument advanced in this chapter is that these forces are changing the nature of competition. They are real, and probably irreversible. However, there is a complex chain to be unravelled and understood if the new role of training and learning in the organisation is to be articulated effectively. This task, though demanding, is essential. The new paradigm of learner-focus cannot be explored, or its implications understood, without an appreciation of the new business forces. Such forces have made organisations re-evaluate how they operate and reconsider the behaviours (or competencies) that they need to instil in their workforce.

Once this is understood, it will be seen that management commitment to the training and learning effort must necessarily be more than lip service. Managers at all levels must be convinced that the time and effort spent is worthwhile and makes business sense.

The new business environment

Although there cannot, at this time of change, be universal agreement on the forces that have created the new business environment, the following factors would appear on most lists:

- globalisation, the opportunity of access to markets through the world, and the fact that new competitors can and will emerge from anywhere

- technology, especially the emergence of the Internet and the widening access to immediate up-to-date information

- consumer expectations, a growing sophistication at all levels and a willingness to change suppliers or demand higher-quality service from public and private sector organisations

- deregulation and liberalisation, the growing refusal of governments to offer protection to producers, and their determination to encourage competition.

The important point about these forces is that they are mutually self-reinforcing. Better and more immediate information creates world markets, which benefit consumers and put pressure on governments. It is not surprising that this has given rise to a whole new set of perspectives on strategy, and some illustrative strands will be considered next.

New perspectives on strategy

Business strategy is concerned with identifying and evaluating the approach that a firm should adopt to compete in the marketplace. Inevitably, perceptions on what constitutes effective strategy have changed as the economy has become more sophisticated. Moreover, different schools emerge and fashions come and go.

Certain trends have become increasingly evident over the last decade. These include a recognition of the limitations of what might be called the low-cost model of competition. Further, there has been a growing interest in resource-based strategy.

Classic approaches to strategy are based in economics. Firms need to be in the right market and adopt an appropriate strategy for that marketplace. Harvard Professor Michael Porter's seminal work[2] *Competitive Strategy* expressed the nature of industry in terms of five forces: threat of entry (new entrants); rivalry among existing competitors; threat of substitute producers and services; bargaining power of suppliers; bargaining power of buyers. Competitive advantage can be seen in terms of relative costs and relative prices which determine profitability. Within this framework three generic strategies can be developed: lower cost, differentiation, and focus. In spite of changing fashions, Porter's underlying analysis is of enduring value: at the end of the day, business success depends on customers who are willing to buy a product which can be produced at a profit.

This truism was starkly underlined by the now notorious dot.com collapse. In March 2000 the

NASDAQ index, which mostly consists of technology and telecom stocks, reached a high of just 5,000 points. In October 2002 it was an astonishing 78 per cent lower. At the time of writing (March 2003) it has recovered slightly and stands at 1,340 points. The frenzied purchasing in 1999 and 2000 of shares in companies launching IPOs (initial public offerings) is well analysed in the aptly titled *Dot.con* by John Cassidy.[3] Investors were anxious not to avoid missing highly promoted opportunities. They therefore invested in companies with limited assets and no prospects of making a profit for years.

In March 2001 Michael Porter wrote an important article in the *Harvard Business Review*. This was intended to serve as a salutary reminder of the fundamentals of effective competition and of the way that they should determine strategy. Porter (2001; pp.63–77) argued that at a time of transition it may appear that new rules of competition are emerging. However, as market rules play themselves out:

> *The creation of true economic value once again becomes the final arbiter of business success*

and

> *Economic value for a company is nothing more than the gap between price and cost, and it is reliably measured only by sustained profitability.*[4]

The way that the Internet may affect competition will be the subject of a later discussion in Chapter 4. First, however, one important implication of this brief overview of traditional strategy needs to be drawn. As Porter put it, potential profitability can be understood only by looking at individual industries and individual companies. When this is undertaken it can be seen that, in certain circumstances, competition through cost is the only viable alternative. The strategy is to become the lowest-cost producer and build profitable business through undercutting the competition. Put simply, no one builds a competitive advantage by offering a higher-value product if they supply plastic bags or metal paint tins. However, in an international market, where labour costs are infinitely cheaper in Eastern Europe and the Far East, it becomes increasingly difficult to build a sustainable competitive advantage through low-cost production. For these reasons the limitations of the low-cost model of competition have become apparent and there has been increasing attention placed on the feasibility and implications of competing by offering consumers a higher-value produce or service.

The emergence of a powerful new strand in strategy analysis, resource-based strategy, is consistent with a move against the low-cost model of competition. It is, however, much more than that and implies a quite different focus. In resource-based approaches to strategy the emphasis is placed on what a company can do rather than on where a company is currently positioned in the marketplace. Organisational strengths are developed, stretched, extended and leveraged for competitive advantage. The aim is to identify and develop distinctive capabilities. These are the factors that differentiate a company from its competitors; they are built up and sustained over time and cannot be easily reproduced by competitors.

A seminal book, which was firmly positioned in resource-based strategy, was produced in 1994 as a transatlantic collaboration by Gary Hamel (of London Business School) and C. K. Prahalad (of the University of Michigan). In *Competing for the Future*[5] they argued that long-term success is about creating unimagined, but soon to be essential, products and services. They observed that similar companies have shown marked differences in resource effectiveness, which could not simply be explained by differences in operational efficiency. Embarking on cost cutting to create leaner organisations is not therefore a long-term answer. Successful companies set ambitious goals and get more out of their resources: they develop particular components of competitor advantage that Hamel and Prahalad called core competencies. They defined core competencies as bundles of skills and technologies that enable a company to provide a particular benefit to customers.

What should be drawn from this brief excursion into strategy is a recognition that the balance has shifted and continues to shift. This is not a consequence of the emergence of the Internet. The Internet may have created both new opportunities and a new urgency. The growing emphasis on competition through people has emerged because of changes in the nature of global competition.

As a consequence, strategies in organisations have become increasingly focused on adding value. Business performance is interpreted more widely – not about short-term financial performance. Value must be delivered to the customer in the long term through quality service, more choice, and an improved experience. In this way repeat business will be secured and corporate reputation enhanced. All this has a profound impact on what is expected (or required) of people who work for the organisation. Their performance is no longer about crude measures of activity (throughput on the production line or calls per hour). Neither is manpower simply a cost to be controlled. Individual behaviour has a profound impact on customer satisfaction.

This has led many organisations across different sectors to rethink their approaches to human resource management and development. The example of INA Bearings set out below offers an illustration of the high-performance working model that is outlined in the next section of this chapter.

CASE STUDY

INA Bearing Company

INA Bearing Company Limited is a subsidiary of a privately owned German engineering group. At its UK manufacturing facility in Llanelli, West Wales, where precision engine components are produced, it employs 360 people.

The business has faced a particularly challenging time. In the 1990s it experienced rapid growth. Over the last three years, the company has been faced with increasing competition from low labour cost countries as group production capacity has been placed in Eastern Europe (Slovakia and Romania) where wages are a fraction of those in the UK.

INA Bearing Company Limited has responded by seeking to compete through developing the capability to deliver higher-value-added products. There has been a planned and sustained focus on continuous improvement, cost reduction and, as an integral component of the process, a sustained attempt to upskill the workforce. As the Personnel Manager, Adrian Roberts puts it:

Previously the investment has been in machinery. Now the investment is in people. You never know what the next product will be, so you need to update the skills so that people have new techniques to cope with whatever comes their way.

The change process began with a management offsite strategy day held in March 2001. The culture change programme developed there identified 'production location of choice' as the vision for the Llanelli plant. 'Integrity, Innovation, Respect, Commitment and Passion' were identified as values. A series of initiatives were put in place on a planned timetable.

The culture change programme involved continuous improvement, training and flexibility; significantly, they were linked and supported by the statement 'The rate of learning must be greater than the rate of change.'

The company felt it important to communicate, as early as possible, the vision and strategy for the future to its employees and so embarked upon a communication exercise whereby a member of the senior management team on an individual basis interviewed each employee.

Guidance for this communication exercise was prepared in the form of a briefing document, to ensure consistency of the message. The guidance note stated that:

- To achieve this vision a 'learning culture' must be at the core of our activities, so that we are practising a culture of continuous improvement and consequently, whatever 'change' is necessary in the future, we have the requisite skills, knowledge and experience to adapt and achieve our targets.

- This will mean the training and development of all people in the organisation to improve our skills knowledge. We will be assessing and appraising everyone within the organisation to ensure that we have a suitably trained and experienced team.

My thanks to Adrian Roberts for his assistance with the preparation of this case study.

High-performance working

By considering the principles of high-performance working it can be seen how appropriate policies and practices could make a difference. Moreover, it can be seen that such policies and practices are desirable in themselves. They can create circumstances in which all parties – employee, employer and external stakeholders – benefit.

High-performance working (HPW) practices are best regarded as new ways of organising work, rewarding performance and involving employees in decision-making. The development of high-performance working organisations (HPWOs) has been advocated by the International Labour Office and by the Chartered Institute of Personnel and Development. A thorough analysis and powerful case for HPWOs was made in a book written by David Ashton and Johnny Sung of the University of Leicester Centre for Labour Market Studies.[6]

In their research Ashton and Sung identify a number of practices that together create HPWOs. For survey purposes they have grouped these practices into four bundles, illustrated in Table 1 below.

Table 1 | Four bundles of high-performance working practices

Work design/employee involvement	Support for performance/training	Rewarding performance	Communication and information sharing
• multi-skilling • quality circles • total quality management • teamworking • self-directed teams	• annual performance reviews • peer reviews/360-degree appraisal • personal development plan • job rotation/cross-training • mentoring • training for trainers	• group-based compensation • profit-sharing • employee share ownership	• regular meetings of the entire workforce • consultative committees • staff attitude surveys

Source: Ashton and Sung *Supporting Workplace Learning for High Performance* (2002); quoted with permission

These bundles of practices were used in the design of a series of international surveys and also in the production of case studies illustrating their application and incidence. Inevitably, a number of qualifications must be made in interpreting the results of research into HPWOs. Not all the practices identified in Table 1 were used in all the national surveys considered by Ashton and Sung. The practices identified in each bundle are not exhaustive. Neither are they all new: some of them (for example job rotation and performance-related pay) have a long-standing history in the interpretation of effective human resources.

What is new, however, is combining these practices in bundles to create a significant positive impact on performance. Ashton and Sung are clear in their conclusion: research in diverse countries has demonstrated a robust link between the use of these bundles of practices and higher levels of productivity and profitability. Moreover, these practices were being implemented effectively in different cultural and institutional contexts and were equally effective in small and large organisations.

On the downside, such working practices are not easy to introduce. They require a high level of trust between managers and employees. Implementation takes time and can be expensive.

Most important, from the perspective of this book, HPW practices are associated with higher levels of learning for all those involved (as can clearly be seen from the INA Bearing Company illustration). The centrality of workplace learning is reflected in the title of Ashton and Sung's book. Employees must be committed to their own personal development and to the acquisition of higher-level technical, interpersonal and problem-solving skills. Although the type of learning will vary depending on the size and circumstances of the company, it does however require a fundamental change of approach to the importance and process of learning in the organisation.

Does human resources make a difference?

High-performance working is an attractive, even compelling, model. Through implementing appropriate and effective human resources policies, it is argued, business success will follow and employees will achieve greater satisfaction. Given this vision, it is scarcely surprising that governments throughout the world are becoming increasingly supportive of high-performance working.

Ultimately, decisions on human resource practice can only be taken in the workplace. Decision-makers in corporate and public sector organisations, whether chief executives, senior managers or (in the case of smaller organisations) owners need to believe that high-performance working is worth the effort. As has been noted, it takes commitment and effort over time to implement HPW practices. These decision-makers need to be convinced that effective human resources, whether expressed in the form of high-performance working practices or otherwise, do indeed make a difference. There is a rich and growing literature emerging in the field of human resources, which serves to demonstrate that effective practices do reflect performance. An important breakthrough was made in 1998 by the US author Jeffrey Pfeffer of Stanford University. In his book *The Human Equation*[7] he argued not only that people were central to success, but that managers could achieve that success by applying a set of seven progressive practices. These he identified as

- employment security
- careful recruitment
- teamwork and decentralisation
- high pay with an incentive element
- extensive training
- narrow status differentials
- lots of communication.

It can be seen that his list of factors corresponds to, but does not duplicate, the HPW list. Frustratingly, but inevitably, all the studies on the impact of human resource practices have taken a slightly different perspective. Important UK research has been commissioned by the CIPD and led by Professor David Guest, currently of Kings College London. In a significant research report published in 2000,[8] 48 separate items were identified as indicators of HR practices. These were placed into the following nine major categories:

- recruitment and selection, training and development
- appraisal
- financial flexibility
- job design
- concern with quality
- communication and consultation

- employment security
- single status
- harmonisation.

Two items were included in each of these two categories, giving a 'short-list' of eighteen indicators of appropriate human resource practices. The research showed that only 1 per cent of the companies surveyed had more than three-quarters of these practices in place and were applying them to most workers. At the other extreme 20 per cent of organisations made extensive use of less than a quarter of these practices. There was a clear association between the number of practices adopted and the effectiveness of these practices. Most importantly, a correlation could be demonstrated between the number of human resource practices in place and profit per employee.

However, a correlation is not the same as a causal link. Because two things move together, it does not necessarily mean that the first causes the second. This point may appear abstruse. In fact it is of considerable importance when examining the connection between effective human resources and business performance. To oversimplify, the correlation is consistent with two quite different explanations: one is that appropriate human resource practices lead to business success; a second is that the implementation of appropriate human resource practices follow from business success (firms have more money to spend on looking after their employees).

There is therefore a need further to explore the linkages between the drivers of business performance and human resource initiatives. This has led to the development by the CIPD and the University of Bath of the People and Performance model, which is considered below. This model sheds important light on the place and role of learning in the modern organisation. It also helps us to begin to answer two important questions.

First, how do people's behaviour and competence impact on operational performance (as defined by the organisation's strategy and objectives)?

Second, what are the most important influences that can bring about these behaviours and develop these competencies?

People and performance

Since 1998 the link between human resource practices and performance has been the subject of ongoing research by the Work and Employment Research Centre at the University of Bath.[9] Their conclusions and the resulting model are outlined in this section. The model is of critical importance for the central arguments advanced in this book. It offers the most credible, relevant and considered framework for a discussion on the contribution of training and learning in the modern organisation. Further, it provides a whole series of valuable insights on how such training and learning interventions can be made most effective.

The research suggest that the crucial factor linking HR practices to performance is the way that these practices lead to discretionary behaviour. This can be defined in the following terms (Purcell, Kinnie, Hutchinson, Rayton and Swart, 2003; p.5):

Discretionary behaviour means making the sort of choices that often define a job, such as the way the job is done – the speed, care, innovation and style of job delivery. This behaviour is at the heart of the employment relationship, because it is hard for the employer to define and then monitor and control the amount of effort, innovation and productive behaviour required. The most obvious example here is front-line service work dealing with customers either face to face or over the phone. It concerns the sort of everyday behaviour that the employer wants but has to rely on the employee to deliver. It may involve emotional labour (smiling down the phone), using knowledge to solve a problem or suggest an alternative to the customer, or it may be internal to the work of the organisation, such as co-operating with team members, helping probationers learn shortcuts or sharing new ideas on work processes. One way or the other, the employee chooses how conscientiously to undertake the job.

Most jobs are built up of many tasks, so the level of complexity can be surprisingly high, even for seemingly routine ones. This choice of how, and how well, to do things is not necessarily made deliberately: it can be unconscious – just part of the way people behave in their organisation. But discretionary behaviour can certainly be withdrawn, often in the sense of adopting an uncaring attitude. This may be a reciprocal response to a belief that 'the firm no longer cares about me, my future or my opinions'.

Ultimately, whatever the incentives or sanctions the firm tries to use, it lies with the employee to 'give' discretionary behaviour and to withdraw it. Although this is described in terms of the action of an individual (we all have bad days), it is the collective withdrawal of discretionary behaviour that is so damaging. Our own experience tells us that there are times when morale is low, or the 'buzz' has gone, or everyone just wants to go home as soon as possible.

The People and Performance model is illustrated diagrammatically in Figure 1. It can be seen to offer a conceptual mapping of key human resource policy areas and to explore their linkage to performance through the discretionary behaviour of individuals and teams. Eleven key human resource areas have been identified in the model. Again these are a slightly different listing from those offered by Ashton and Sung for their HPW work, and from Pfeffer and from Guest *et al*, which were considered in the previous section of this chapter.

At the heart of the model is a central block showing what encourages people to exercise discretionary behaviour, experience job satisfaction and become motivated and committed to the organisation. This central block is what Purcell and colleagues refer to as AMO – ability, motivation and opportunity. For employees, individually and collectively, to engage in the sort of discretionary behaviour that is beneficial to the firm, the three conditions of AMO must apply: there must be enough employees with the necessary ability (skills, experience, knowledge) to do current, and perhaps, future jobs; there must be adequate motivation for them to apply their abilities; they must be given the opportunity by their co-workers and their immediate bosses. As Purcell *et al* (2003; p.6) explain:

- The assumption in A (Ability) is that people will want to apply for jobs in an organisation (recruitment), have their attributes recognised (selection) and be willing to learn new skills and behaviours (training and development).

- In M (Motivation) the assumption is that people can be motivated to use their ability

Figure 1 | *The People and Performance model*

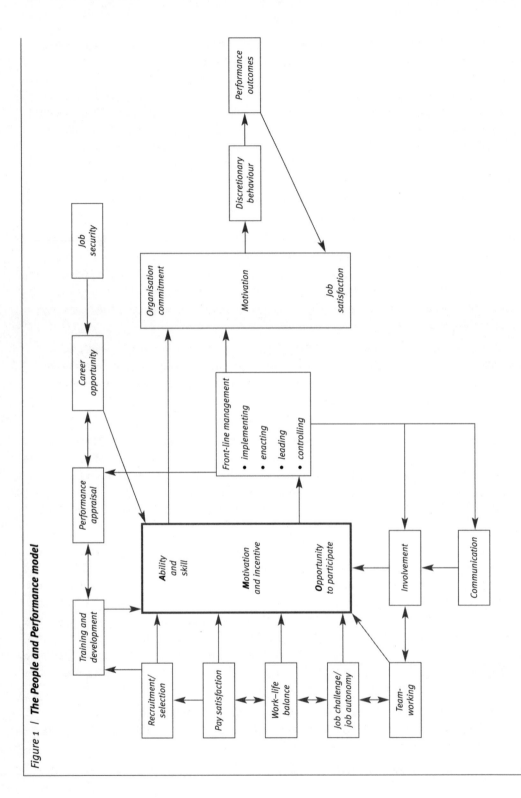

in a productive manner because they will respond to various extrinsic and intrinsic rewards and stimuli.

- In O (Opportunity) the assumption is that people will provide good customer service, or high-quality work beyond the satisfactory level, and will wish to engage in problem-solving or wider involvement schemes, given the opportunities to do so. They need the opportunity both to use or practise their skills and contribute to collective efforts at the team, section and organisation level. In other words, to have the opportunity to participate in these efforts both in doing their job and in the organisation.

Employers thus need to have some basic AMO policies in order to meet minimum industry standards for survival, but effective firms have a level of sophistication in their approach to people management which helps induce discretionary behaviour and above-average performance.

The People and Performance research has involved a series of interviews with employees and managers. Seven hundred were conducted. The linkages, their importance, and the precise effect of the eleven human resource policies varied by company according to the type of employee and the history and culture of the firm.

However, there is increasing scope for discretionary behaviour and it is gaining importance, since (CIPD 'Research Summary',[10] 2002; p.2):

The growth of the service economy, knowledge work and work transformations in manufacturing all point to the centrality of discretionary behaviour and thus the need to manage it.

'Work transformations in manufacturing' can be read as equivalent to the introduction of high-performance working. Discretionary behaviour, then, leads to favourable performance outcomes, which can produce profitability in the corporate sector and service outcomes in the voluntary and public sectors.

Effective performance from people

An immediate question, in the context of this book, is to ask what part is played by training and learning in the People and Performance model. This will be the subject of the final section of this chapter. First, however, a further consideration of aspects of the model is needed if training and learning are to be put into an appropriate context.

The research that underpins the People and Performance model evidently opens up exciting possibilities. It offers some answers to what have been described as 'black box' questions: these concern the often unclear processes that occur when inputs (eg labour and capital) are converted into useful outputs (eg profit and productivity). It becomes possible to move beyond general statements like 'people are our most important assets' and take action to create the conditions that produce the desired outcomes.

What the People and Performance model offers is the idea that such actions should be designed to produce appropriate discretionary behaviour. There are both short-term implications and long-term implications. The behaviour of the individual line managers, further explored below, is critical in creating the short-term climate. A focus on the longer term brings us into a discussion of what has become known as the psychological contract.

The underlying idea of the psychological contract is straightforward: work represents a deal between employer and employee in which each makes explicit or implicit commitments to the other. A simple description is 'the perceptions of both parties to the employment relationship, organisation and individual, of the obligations implied in that relationship (Herriot and Pemberton,[11] 1997; pp.45–46). If both sides honour the deal, displaying and earning trust, a positive psychological contract is maintained. However, the breach of the psychological contract by the employer (and equally the employee) can lead to negative consequences and damage both employee satisfaction and commitment. This is a breach of trust, and one obvious consequence is the withdrawal of discretionary effort.

The role of line managers is critical in maintaining a healthy psychological contract. A well-worn adage of modern human resources is 'people don't leave organisations, they leave bosses'. As can be seen from Figure 1, line managers have a pivotal position in the People and Performance model. To quote from the summary of the research (p.4):

> *Line managers apply most policies and practices related to people management. This has become more pronounced in recent years with the shift towards individualism in the employment relationship and the trend towards devolving the application of HR management to the line. Increasingly it is these managers who are relied upon to 'bring policies to life' as one of our senior managers put it.*

and

> *This type of behaviour – the way immediate line managers and team leaders manage their staff (and the way they themselves are managed) – is itself discretionary. Managers vary, of course, but how much attention is given to the way managers deal with people management issues is itself a reflection of what they are allowed and encouraged to do.*

These strands – high-performance working, the impact of human resources, policies and practice, people and performance, the psychological contract and line managers – can be seen to reinforce a single thread. People are indeed the most important assets. Perhaps this should be stated more precisely as 'committed individuals who understand the organisation's objectives, have the requisite skills, and operate in an environment where they have the opportunity to take the appropriate discretionary behaviour, create powerful business advantages which can be very difficult for a competitor to duplicate'. (This is the author's own articulation.)

Resource-based strategy shifts the focus from the external market to the internal competencies based in people and technology. Appropriate discretionary behaviour lies at the heart of the new approaches to competition. The aim is to create an organisation composed of self-confident individuals who are seeking to acquire the requisite knowledge and skills to enable them to meet customer/client requirements and advance the organisation's goals and objectives. The human resources function, then, does indeed make a difference, but in complex ways. The crucial contribution of human resource interventions lies in the creation of an environment that encourages appropriate behaviour by the employee and develops his or her potential to behave in this way. It is against this background that training and learning can be considered.

The role of training, learning and development

So what part does the systematic enhancement of knowledge and skills play in developing a competitive approach which reflects the new perspectives? A superficial analysis of the People and Performance model could suggest that training and development is just one of a number of necessary inputs. It carries the same weight as, say, the provision of appropriate systems of communication or the guarantee of job security.

This would be a mistake. What is required in the model is the creation of a virtuous circle of best-practice human resources which is sustained over the long term and is self-reinforcing. Effective training and development should not be regarded as simply an independent variable, which adds just one of a number of valuable ingredients.

This is not to say that formal training and development (the term used in the Bath study) policies are not important in their own right. The research undertaken by Bath considered a wide range of organisations: large and small, public sector and private sector. Training and development (and also performance appraisal) emerged as a powerful positive influence in every case. Put simply, if individuals are satisfied with training and development, then their commitment, motivation and job satisfaction are significantly higher. There is therefore clear evidence to support the assertion that appropriate training and development policies should not only be put in place, but they should be communicated effectively. Employees should know that the organisation takes training and development seriously.

However, training and learning is about much more than formal policies: it is more than one variable among many. A moment's reflection shows that it pervades the model and is integral to the whole process.

Consider, for example, the following list taken from the People and Performance research report (p.71).

Particularly important policies and practices which came through in our statistical analysis and are seen in our case studies are:

- *opportunities for career advancement*
- *doing a challenging job*
- *having some influence on how the job is done*
- *opportunities for training*
- *having a say in decisions which affect my job*
- *working in teams*
- *working for a firm which assists people to balance home and work*
- *being able to raise matters of concern*
- *having a boss who respects me*
- *having managers who are good at leadership.*

More generally, one of the most powerful ideas which drives modern management thinking is a recognition that well-trained line managers are critical to the delivery of effective human resources. Ultimately, they are the ones who motivate staff directly, who give them an opportunity to participate, and create the required climate of trust. Above all they are the ones who will coach, identify skills needs, encourage development, and find the time for their staff to participate in training. It will be the line manager who will create the opportunity for the individual employee to take the appropriate initiative. Certainly it will be the line manager who will signal whether that behaviour is welcome. The negative side is that line managers can certainly kill initiative.

One other consequence of the model needs to be considered. It reintroduces the central theme of the book. Increasingly the interventions or activities designed to improve knowledge and skills will be about learning and not training.

This transition from training to learning is entirely consistent with the emphasis on discretionary behaviour. If employees are encouraged to exercise appropriate initiative, seeking to acquire and develop the knowledge and skills to do their current and future jobs must be seen as a particularly welcome way in which they exercise that discretion. Learning, as was argued in the Introduction to this book, lies in the domain of the individual. Employees can be made to attend training courses; they cannot be made to learn skills. Certainly, in no sense can they be made actively to seek learning opportunities. The growing importance of learning is widely recognised and well understood by most training professionals. The need to articulate it explicitly in models is considered in Chapter 2. In this chapter and throughout the book 'learning and training' rather than 'training and learning' will be used to emphasise the primacy of the former.

REFERENCES AND READING

1   The Investors in People standard was developed in 1990. It provides a flexible framework for organisations to develop best practice in people management. www.investorsinpeople.co.uk

2   PORTER, M. E. (1980) *Competitive Strategy: Techniques for analysing industries and competitors*. New York, Free Press.

3   CASSIDY, J. (2002) *Dot.con*. New York, Collins; London, Allen Lane The Penguin Press.

4   PORTER, M. E. (2001) 'Strategy and the Internet', *Harvard Business Review,* March. Reprinted by kind permission of *Harvard Business Review*. From 'Strategy and the Internet' by M. E. Porter, March 2001. Copyright © 2001 by the Harvard Business School Publishing Corporation; all rights reserved.

5   HAMEL, G. and PRAHALAD, C. K. (1994) *Competing for the Future*. Boston, Harvard Business School Press.

6   ASHTON, D. A. and SUNG, J. (2002) *Supporting Workplace Learning for High Performance Working*. Geneva, International Labour Office.

7   PFEFFER, J. (1998) *The Human Equation: Building profits by putting people first*. Boston, Harvard Business School Press.

8   GUEST, D., MICHIE, J., SHEEHAN, M., CONWAY, C. and METOCHI, M. (2000) *Effective People Management*. CIPD Research Report. London, the CIPD.

9   PURCELL, J., KINNIE, N., HUTCHINSON, S., RAYTON, B. and SWART, J. (2003) *Understanding the People and Performance Link: Unlocking the Black Box*. CIPD Research Report. London, the CIPD. See

also Purcell, J., Kinnie, N. and Hutchinson, S. (2003) 'Open minded', *People Management*, Vol 9, No. 10, 15 May; pp.30–37.

10 CIPD (2002) *Sustaining Success in Difficult Times.* CIPD Research Summary. London, the CIPD.

11 Herriot, P. and Pemberton, C. (1997) 'Facilitating new deals', *Human Resource Management*, Vol 7, No. 1; pp.45–56.

2

The place of models

Some of the Business Heads emerged as supportive, helpful and positive in their outlook. One in particular, however, remained an absolute nightmare. His underlying position was that he was entirely in favour of training and development provided he or his senior team didn't have to do anything. That was HR's job. One day I received an unexpected summons to a meeting in his office. I arrived, fearing the worst, and found a man transformed. 'How are we getting on with staff development, and am I and my team doing enough to assist?' was his opening. I first assumed that he had been captured by an alien intelligence that had placed another being in his body. I then spotted a figure in the corner taking extensive notes on a clipboard. The unreconstructed Business Head was being assessed by an observer as part of a high-level competency profiling exercise. He knew what the correct behaviour was and, totally out of character, had decided to display it.

This chapter will consider some important implications that follow from the transition to learning from training. It will begin the discussion of the mindset required if training professionals are to grasp the new opportunities to assist this process. Then a review of the role and value of models will be presented. Two dominant models (systematic training and the learning organisation) will be discussed. This will be followed by a consideration of newly emerging ideas: called, for short, convergence models. The chapter will end with a further consideration of the learner-focus paradigm and its consequences.

First, however, it is helpful to consider some further research input. Again this was undertaken by the Bath team as part of the CIPD People and Performance study. This aspect considered smaller 'knowledge-intensive firms'. The findings are outlined in the case study below. The extent to which such practices represent the way of the future is debatable. Larger organisations in the public, manufacturing and service sectors may well continue to operate quite differently from these smaller more specialised players. However, the tendencies evident in these knowledge-intensive firms represent a major challenge to our traditional view of learning and training. They again draw our attention to the ongoing, often informal, activities that lead to learning, as opposed to the deliberate interventions that constitute training.

Learning in knowledge-intensive firms

In 2001 and 2002 the Bath team undertook research into six knowledge-intensive firms (or KIFs). This study formed an important element of the People and Performance project. Their results were published in 2003 (Swart, Kinnie and Purcell, 2003[1]). In these organisations the knowledge of the workforce is inextricably linked with the product or service offered to customers or clients. Law and accounting firms, management, engineering and computer consultancy companies, advertising agencies, research and development units and high-tech companies are examples. Work in these firms is of an intellectual nature and well-educated qualified employees form a major part of the workforce. In summary, these are organisations which (Swart *et al*, 2003; p.ix):

> *employ a high proportion of knowledge workers, are engaged in work which applies expertise to novel problems, and provide services for business clients, sometimes in collaboration with an external network.*

These organisations rely on knowledge held and applied by the employees; three applications of knowledge were seen as critical to success. These were: developing individual knowledge and skills; sharing and developing this knowledge within the organisation; sharing and developing this knowledge with clients and other parties in the network.

It would be expected that human resource processes (or people management, the term used in the report) would play a critical role in such organisations. Given the nature of the organisations and the way in which they compete, three human resource policies and practices were of particular importance. One concerned the recruitment, development and reward of individuals; a second concerned the facilitation of knowledge sharing within the organisation; a third concerned developing and managing relationships, clients and other parties.

The study found some tensions in such organisations. There was a need to manage the tensions that were (*ibid.*):

> *created between the needs of knowledge workers and the requirement to share knowledge between competing team, organisational, professional and client loyalty or identities, and between the need for formal HR policies and more informal approaches to the management of employees.*

These tensions were overcome, in successful firms, through ensuring that people were managed in a way that supported and enhanced practices and processes for developing and sharing knowledge. In short, such firms develop their capability by achieving a mutually supportive HR advantage.

The implications for our view of human resources are considerable. It seems that a new approach is emerging in knowledge-intensive firms: effective human resources plays a key role in developing the kind of capital that these firms need in order to acquire business and manage customer relationships. People management practices are inextricably linked with the business model.

Inevitably all this has considerable implications for the form of learning and training that takes place. The following illustrative quotations capture some key points:

> *Tacit skill accumulation at individual level through learning-by-doing was also supported by such measures as a formalised mentoring system and performance management systems. Both these types of system were used to encourage learning and to enforce the behavioural norms in the organisation.*
>
> (p.37)

> *The focal point of learning individually through reflection on the project or acquiring organisation-specific skills through observing others is that the behavioural dimensions of the skills cannot be verbalised.*
>
> (p.37)

> *The sharing of information was combined with practice: by directly showing fellow knowledge workers how to practise a skill or by providing advice intermittently during the application of a skill.*
>
> (p.38)

> *It was grounded upon a shared understanding of what the skill is. The social construction of competence though working together closely over an extended period of time was therefore important to knowledge sharing.*
>
> (p.38)

Generally in the KIFs there was an unbreakable link between learning and knowledge development – the two could not be separated as a concept or in practice. Group and team learning was pervasive. There was much emphasis on the developmental aspects of performance appraisals. Mentoring and coaching were used extensively, and there was emphasis on developmental assignments designed to stretch the individual. Consideration was given to the provision of time to learn and, in at least one case, the opportunity to acquire new knowledge was given as a reward for effective performance.

Learning took place across the supply chain through knowledge development and exchange with suppliers and customers. Overall, in many different respects boundaries were disappearing. Knowledge management blurred into learning and learning activities crossed organisations.

> *More generally, this research demands a rethink of the relationship between training and knowledge management. If sharing of knowledge is the key to organisational success, the training professional will need to have thought through the way in which his or her activities can contribute to that process.*

In these knowledge-intensive firms there is unquestionably a shift to learning from training and much more emphasis on individual responsibility for learning. In these organisations a focus on the learner is happening in practice. Formal instructor-led training, delivered internally, is not seen as important. As the study report puts it (p.37):

> *Taught training courses were therefore of little value and it was only the sharing of experience in different communities within the organisation and with the client that laid a solid foundation for knowledge creation.*

So, in some circumstances at least, the new paradigm of learner-focus may be of value. This may be particularly true, as seen in the case study above, when there is a close link between learning and knowledge management. Since this term will be used on many occasions later in this book, it may be helpful to offer a definition at this stage. The term 'knowledge management' emerged, and achieved rapid popularity, in the 1990s. Many definitions have been offered reflecting different perspectives in its constitution and how it should be embedded in an organisation. Knowledge management is essentially a systematic process of finding, sharing and using data to enhance an organisation's objectives.[2] Technology has made this increasingly feasible, and many knowledge-intensive organisations have developed databases which allow them to create and share information by placing material or 'objects' in repositories. These can then be accessed and used by others. Other commentators have stressed the softer skills involved in knowledge management – the need to create a collaborative culture.

The role of technology will be considered in Chapters 4 and 5 of this book. First, however, having recognised that a shift to learning from training is a reality for at least some organisations, it is appropriate to consider the role of paradigms and models.

Why bother with models?

In the Introduction to this book a focus on the learner was described as a paradigm. This is a conceptual framework in which theories are constructed; it is a way of looking at the world. 'Paradigm shift' was identified as a phrase used describe the traumatic changes that can result from a new discovery. The classic illustration of a paradigm shift was the recognition that the world was round, not flat: this demanded a whole new view on geography with its consequent impact on the way that commerce could be conducted.

A model is also a mental construct. It can be defined in a variety of ways, but one expression appears in most dictionaries: 'an object of imitation' (*Oxford English Dictionary*) or 'something to be copied' (*Chambers Dictionary*). Moving beyond the physical form (the artist's model), in this sense a model can also be viewed as a 'pattern of excellence' (a phrase which is also included in Chambers' definition).

The brief discussion of models that follows may appear unduly academic. It is offered partly to introduce the critique of the systematic training model which follows immediately below. However, it is to be hoped that a discussion on models is not dismissed as an esoteric sideline by thinking practitioners for the following reasons.

First, the central thesis of this book is that the aspirational paradigm of learner-focus offers a new opportunity for the training professional. If it is to move from aspiration to reality, there is a need to construct new models. This can only be achieved if there is a clarity of intention.

The second reason is that periodically it is sensible to ask what one is doing and why. This process is assisted by models. Training professionals can understandably be absorbed with the immediate requirements of their job and might rather not put aside time for reflection. Given the current turbulent change, a review of models, and in particular the systematic training model, is timely.

It is therefore useful to consider what a model is, and how and whether it could and should be used. If a wider view is taken of the definition of a model, it can be argued that a model has a number of potential uses: it can be a form of description; it can be a theory; it can be an expression of belief; it can be a signal of best practice. Each will be outlined briefly in turn below.[3]

- 'A model as description' is the simplest of the concepts. Here the suggestion is that actions that are taking place, and are observable, can best be explained in terms of a model. This is easy to express in the world of training and development. Here we are saying that things are happening because trainers are seeking to act in accordance with the implications of a certain model.

- 'A model as theory' is a looser concept. Here it is recognised that certain actions are taking place in organisations on a considered basis. They can be best explained in terms of a model, although those who are undertaking the actions, those who are making the interventions, may not consider that they are working in accordance with a model, not appreciate the need for a model, nor even find it of value if they were given an outline. They are taking actions that they think are appropriate in themselves, but are not acting within the guidelines of a predetermined model. Both of these uses of the term 'model' are practical: they are about actions.

- 'A model as expression of belief' is an entirely different concept. It has a normative dimension. The view here is that it would be a good thing (for the individual, the organisation or even humankind in general) if this model were adopted. It states that 'this is the way that things ought to be done'. It extends beyond practical considerations of efficiency. It is subtly different from the fourth category of model.

- 'A model as a signal of best practice': this last is more pragmatic. What is said here is that best practice is in fact taking place when people are acting in accordance with the model.

Each of these ways of using the term 'model' can be of value. It can be useful to have a way of categorising and explaining actions ('model as description' or 'model as theory') and to have a basis for advocating and bringing about better practice ('model as expression of belief' and 'model as a signal of best practice'). What is important, however, in promoting the concept of the model is to be clear what you are using it for and why. Against this background, it is appropriate to review the predominant models that have influenced the training profession.

The systematic training model

The systematic training model became increasingly accepted in late 1960s on both sides of the Atlantic. In the USA it has been embedded in the syllabuses of universities and colleges who teach a subject known as Instructional Systems Design. In the UK it often appears as the basis of recommended tools for trainers. The various industry training boards established by the Industrial Training Act 1964 all advocated in some form or other in their literature an approach which they labelled the systematic training model.

Essentially, it was thought appropriate to regard training as a series of sequential steps or stages. In the simplest expressions of the systematic training model, these steps were:

- identifying training needs
- designing training
- delivering training
- evaluating training outcomes.

Other expressions were extensions or developments of this basic sequence.

Two examples are illustrated. The first (shown as Figure 2) is the model in its most basic, simplest form. The second (shown as Figure 3) is taken from a 1998 report by the American Society for Training and Development (ASTD) on the impact of learning technology on the activities undertaken by HR professionals. This latter expresses the ISD model in terms of learning technology.[4]

In whatever form it is expressed the systematic training model has two important characteristics. First, as has been noted, it offers a series of consecutive, but linked, interventions; second, the identification of needs is something that can be introduced into the training cycle at the appropriate stage. These needs are discovered by carrying out a thorough investigation of individual or group training requirements, by interpreting the overall objectives set by the organisation, or by a well-managed combination of the two.

Figure 2 / **The systematic training model**

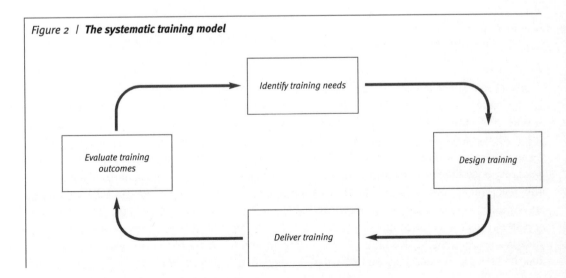

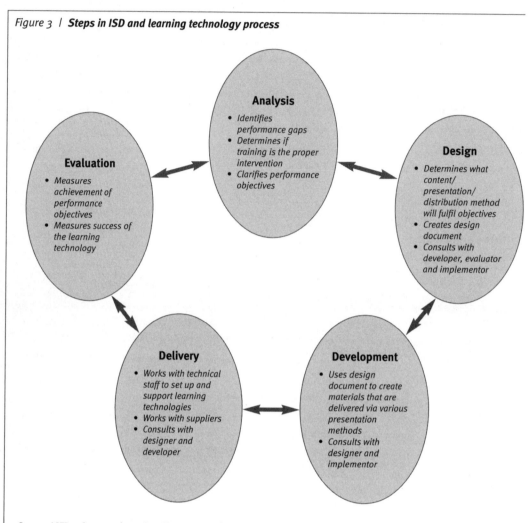

Figure 3 / **Steps in ISD and learning technology process**

Analysis
- Identifies performance gaps
- Determines if training is the proper intervention
- Clarifies performance objectives

Evaluation
- Measures achievement of performance objectives
- Measures success of the learning technology

Design
- Determines what content/ presentation/ distribution method will fulfil objectives
- Creates design document
- Consults with developer, evaluator and implementor

Delivery
- Works with technical staff to set up and support learning technologies
- Works with suppliers
- Consults with designer and developer

Development
- Uses design document to create materials that are delivered via various presentation methods
- Consults with designer and implementor

Source: ASTD, reference 4 (reproduced by permission)

Considered against the background of the discussion of the new competitive forces, a number of challenges can be raised. The systematic training model is a construct that was developed at a time when the training manager saw his or her role as intervention to support the organis-ation. Nowadays, a more proactive involvement is expected of the training specialist. As has been illustrated in the consideration of knowledge-intensive firms, individuals are expected to take responsibility for their own learning and managers are expected to take responsibility for the development of their staff. The front-end questions to start the process are best articulated as 'What do I need to learn?' or 'How can I help my staff develop?' rather than 'What does the business need now?' Such questions are critical in organisations where people are expected to take more responsibility for their personal contribution to business performance. The answers may be less precise and less well articulated: they are much more intuitive.

This modern approach to competition requires the sustained development of a self-confident and self-aware workforce. Learning and training are a continuous part of the process and an ongoing activity – hence the emergence of the term 'learning organisation', which will be considered later in this chapter. It is a proactive process, almost an act of faith and commitment. To wait until a business need is identified before setting training objectives and undertaking design and development is inappropriate.

Some additional strands are emerging from this brief overview of the systematic training model. They concern first, the idea that training is best seen as a series of interventions, and second, that the trainer is the person who should be leading/directing or organising these interventions.

The shift to learning from training demands a thorough reconsideration of the place of interventions. Interventions are intended to alter the pattern of activities that would otherwise take place in the organisation. It is easy to think in terms of training interventions (guiding managers in the conduct of a performance appraisal system and helping them acquire the necessary skills, for example), but the concept of a 'learning intervention' is far more elusive.

However, it may be elusive but it is not impossible. A first suggestion is that a training manager must intervene to promote learning in two respects. First, he or she can undertake some activities to assist the individual learner. Second, he or she can act to manage the climate and context in which learning can take place.

An illustration of the first type of intervention is to consider what can be called the 'learning cycle' as opposed to the training cycle. Figure 4 is taken from a 1999 publication *Managing Learning for Added Value* (Guile and Fonda, 1999[5]; p.22). Given this perspective, the trainer's role becomes one of facilitating individuals and managers through what can be regarded as a series of 'front-end' questions. The starting point, when individuals take personal responsibility, is the question 'What difference could my learning make to my performance, and as a result, to the performance of the business?' This whole topic will be explored further in the third Part of the book where the role of the trainer is reviewed.

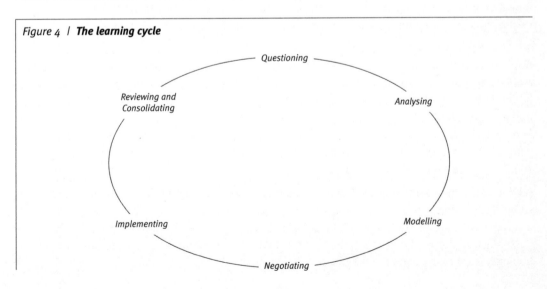

*Figure 4 | **The learning cycle***

Questioning

Reviewing and
Consolidating

Analysing

Implementing

Modelling

Negotiating

The six stages of the cycle are:

Questioning:
exploring my understanding of the outcomes and behaviour that a situation or challenge requires, and calling into question aspects of organisational practice and existing wisdom that may limit my capability to take responsibility for these.

Analysing:
working with my manager and others to explore learning needs in relation to my capability.

Modelling:
working with my manager and others to identify the types of learning opportunities that could help me to develop the behaviours I need.

Negotiating:
agreeing rights and responsibilities in support of behavioural change (a 'learning plan').

Implementing:
all parties fulfilling their contribution to meeting the objectives of the 'learning plan'.

Reviewing and Consolidating:
following through on the broader organisational implications of the 'learning plan', and developing new forms of practice.

Before leaving this consideration of systematic training, however, one other issue should be considered. Set against the background of the discussion at the beginning of this chapter, what sort of model is systematic training? A depressing conclusion is that this discussion has not received sufficient attention: the systematic training model has gained acceptance without adequate debate on its place. It is hard to argue that it is a 'model as description' or 'model as theory'. If it were to be either of these, it would need to be seen as a far more rigorous construct and pervasive in its application. One of the features of the model is sufficient to raise many doubts. As will be seen in Chapter 8, evaluation practice has been a major area of concern and repeated evidence suggests that insufficient evaluation is taking place. If evaluation is not taking place on a systematic basis, it cannot be said that the systematic training model is governing practice.

Any review of the literature will show that the systematic training model is advanced as a normative concept – it is something that 'ought' to be taking place. It is a 'model as expression of belief' or 'as a signal of best practice'. It continually appears in various government-sponsored initiatives as an indicator of what organisations ought to be doing (for example, in Investors in People and the National Training Awards). If it is used in this way, the model is potentially dangerous. Learning and training have moved over the last 40 years and new models are needed which are based on the new paradigm.

All the above may seem unduly harsh on the systematic training model. There is considerable value in applying a disciplined and structured approach to training. This is particularly true when a problem is well defined and the population large and clearly identified. This explains the emergence of the model in the military context where, for example, a considerable amount of equipment training needs to take place.

The problem is that the systematic training model has become more than it should be. There is a danger that it can act as a barrier to the further development of ideas.

The learning organisation

Such has been the pervasiveness of the systematic training model that other perspectives on training seem almost peripheral by comparison. One model which did achieve a degree of prominence, however, was the learning organisation.

The interest in the concept of the learning organisation can be dated to the publication in 1990 of a book by the US commentator Peter Senge.[6] Senge differentiated learning organisations from traditional authoritarian 'controlling organisations'. He argued that a number of new 'component technologies' or disciplines were converging to innovate learning organisations – the most important of which was 'systems thinking', the capacity for putting things together and seeking holistic solutions.

Senge wrote a stimulating, complex and demanding book. His thoughts on team learning and the way that this created organisational advantage were of immense value. The concept of the learning organisation excited many practitioners and gave rise to a plethora of books, articles and conferences on the learning organisation. However, interest in the concept has declined markedly since the late 1990s.[7]

One reason for the decline is that the learning organisation was always a loose, ill-defined concept. It failed to become grounded in reality and was quite simply overtaken by events. Multiple definitions of the term 'learning organisation' were offered. Most seemed to begin with the assumption that learning was a good thing, and that organisations should promote individual and organisational learning. What was lacking was a clear agreement on the steps that should be taken to make this happen and the climate in which it could take root.

So what sort of model was the learning organisation, if indeed it was a model at all? There is a worthwhile case to be made that the learning organisation was a paradigm, a way of looking at the world, which was ahead of its time. If so, its decline is to be lamented. However, when considered as a model it can only be categorised as 'a model as expression of belief'. Certainly for many of its advocates, including government organisations, there was a distinct flavour of 'Wouldn't it be nice if the world was like this?' in the literature. We will return to this discussion in the final section of this chapter.

Convergence models

This general heading is used to describe some emerging strands or trends which may or may not in time amount to a new model. They are about a convergence of interventions in the organisation. They all seek to maximise the effectiveness of the individual in doing his or her job. They recognise the new opportunities for technology to make information or support directly available to individuals. They all mark a shift away from seeing training as an isolated activity.

In the USA the term 'human performance improvement' (HPI) is becoming more widely used. In part this is due to advocacy by the American Society for Training and Development (ASTD). In introducing a HPI Certificate Program, the ASTD President and CEO Tina Sung argued that 'All over the world, the shift from training to performance improvement is accelerating. Business leaders expect training and performance solutions to be linked in their organisation's strategies and bottom line measures.' Accordingly, HPI was defined as 'the systematic process of articulating organisation goals, relating these goals to the performance of people, uncovering the reasons for performance gaps, implementing solutions, managing change and evaluating the direct and indirect results'.[8]

Indeed, the ASTD's view that training, learning and performance improvement are inextricably linked is reflected in the term 'workplace learning and performance profession' when it issues attendance certificates at conferences. It has published a book designed to assist 'seasoned training professionals who wish to make the transition to HPI'.[9] HPI is described as results-based, 'driven by a business need and a performance need' which always works in the following sequence (Sanders, 2002; p.4):

- Identify an organisational problem.
- Articulate a relationship between the problem and human performance.
- Determine a quantifiable performance gap between the desired level of performance and the actual level of performance.
- Conduct an analysis of the root causes to reveal the reasons for the performance gap.
- Implement a series of solutions to address the root causes.

Such solutions should extend beyond learning and training interventions, which could be necessary components, but must be fully integrated.

The increasing power of technology makes integrated solutions far more feasible. This has been recognised by the IT companies themselves who are increasingly interested in the possibilities of providing multi-faceted packages. Sun Microsystems, for example, is currently developing and advocating an approach they call 'Enterprise Talent Management',[10] which they advocate in the following terms:

> *Technology has done a good job of delivering comprehensive, enterprise-strength solutions for supply chain management, enterprise resource planning and lately customer resource management, but not yet for people, learning, skills and knowledge management. In the next two years, however, you can expect the gap to be filled through enterprise talent management systems.*

> *Enterprise talent management – the application of integrated technologies for developing people, skills, learning and knowledge management – is predicted to be the next big area of growth in technology solutions for enterprises.*

Although they are at an early stage of development, it is possible to regard such approaches as an example of 'models as an expression of belief' or 'as a signal of best practice'.

Models and the learner-focus

Some clear patterns emerge from this brief consideration of models. First, most models lie in the normative or 'ought to' category. They are predominantly models as expressions of belief. Whether they are articulated by government, a training organisation or, as in the last example, a provider of IT solutions, they are put forward in the belief that this is what trainers ought to be doing.

To re-emphasise, this use of a model is perfectly legitimate. The government is concerned with the need to update workplace skills for economic and social reasons. If it believes that this could be achieved if all organisations were to deliver training interventions using the systematic training model as a guide, it is correct to advocate it. However, since it has been around for some time, there is bound to be a lot of institutional attachment to such a model, and this can discourage questions on its legitimacy.

A central argument of this book is that we are undergoing a period of uncertainty and turbulence. If this is accepted as true, 'models as expressions of belief' should be treated with caution. Moreover, it has been argued that the turbulence is marked by a shift of focus from training to learning. This raises a further set of questions on models. With the exception of the learning organisation (which it was argued was ahead of its time and insufficiently grounded), the emphasis in the models considered has been on the actions that should be taken by bodies other than the learner. The systematic training model and its variants advocates the steps that training professionals should take to ensure that training interventions are appropriate and effective. There is nothing wrong with this as such. It has its place. It is simply a limited aim for an organisation which wishes to encourage learning.

The challenge now is to develop, articulate and promote new models, approaches, ways of working (whatever terminology is preferred) and implement them in organisations. Such approaches should now consist of actions or interventions taken against the background of the new aspirational paradigm of a focus on the learner. This paradigm was first presented in the Introduction to the book and is reproduced below:

> *Interventions and activities which are intended to improve knowledge and skills in organisations will increasingly focus on the learner. Emphasis will shift to the individual learner (or the team), and he or she will be encouraged to take more responsibility for his or her learning. Efforts will be made to develop a climate which supports effective and appropriate learning. Such interventions and activities will form part of an integrated approach to creating competitive advantage through people in the organisation.*

These interventions, once identified and developed, could then constitute a model, and moreover a model in the sense of a signal of best practice. This, as has been noted, is a pragmatic expression of the term 'model'. The underlying argument runs as follows. Those responsible for developing the workforce in organisations should recognise and understand the forces that have brought about the shift in focus from learning to training. Most importantly, they should interpret the consequences of this shift in the context of their organisations. They should therefore act in a way that develops individual and team learning so that they contribute more effectively to develop business performance. Such actions will be concerned with the deployment of time and/or money, which are the two key resources available.

The effective identification of such interventions and actions is the major challenge facing those involved in organisational learning and training (called, for short, the 'training professional'). To underline again the central theme, this requires a new mindset.

For some the idea of 'learner-centred interventions' may cause problems. It may appear to be an oxymoron, something which tries to combine contradictory terms. By its very nature learning is personal, self-directed, experiential – no one can do it for you. It is, however, possible for organisations to put in place policies and systems that encourage people to learn, as a con-sideration of the 'learning cycle' set out in Figure 4 illustrates. However, in order to do this it is necessary to have a wide understanding of how people learn in organisations. This will form the subject of the next chapter.

Some concluding comments are needed before moving into this discussion. The first involves a return to the term 'learning organisation'. Advocates of this concept, and there are many, might argue that the paradigm of learner-focus is no more than a revision of the 'learning organisation' from a different perspective. There is some justice in this assertion. Action is much more import-ant than semantics. If, in taking the appropriate actions, a training professional argues that he or she is creating a learning organisation, that is his or her choice. However, what is proposed in this book takes advantage of the entirely new possibilities created by technology (the subject of Chapters 4 and 5). These have arisen since the term 'learning organisation' fell into decline. Further, it is essential that such activities are firmly grounded in the realities of the organisation if the current window of opportunity is to be grasped. We must move beyond a model expression of belief. Implementing a focus on the learner is not something that is desirable; it is something that must be done.

This chapter ends with a table setting out some factors that should be considered in designing interventions that emphasise learning, not training. This is presented as Table 2. It is con-structed from the organisation's perspective: for the organisation it is desirable that employees learn certain knowledge and skills. If this is to happen, if effective learning is to take place, a number of dimensions need to be considered. Four main headings are presented in the table: the links with the business, the scope of the application, the type of knowledge, and the prior position of the learner. This list must be interpreted and refined in the context of any particular situation. What is important to note is that the approach is far removed from traditional training models.

Table 2 | A framework for interventions

Links with the business	Scope of application	Type of knowledge	Position of learner
• importance of the topic • urgency of requirements (speed to market) • what, exactly, are we seeking to learn?	• specific to the business • general to all organisations	• abstract (content intensive) • practical (skills intensive)	• extent of prior knowledge/ awareness • motivation of learner • support structure available

REFERENCES AND READING

1 SWART, J., KINNIE, N. and PURCELL, J. (2003) *People and Performance in Knowledge Intensive Firms*. CIPD Research Report. London, the CIPD.

2 Professor Harry Scarbrough, now of Warwick University, discussed knowledge management more fully in SCARBROUGH, H., SWAN, J. and PRESTON, J. (1999) *Knowledge Management: A literature review*. London, IPD.

3 I am grateful to George Mitchell for his insights, which greatly assisted the arguments presented in this section.

4 PISKURICH, G. M. and SANDERS, E. S. (1998) *Models for Learning Technologies: Roles, competencies and outputs*. Alexandria, Virginia, American Society for Training and Development.

5 GUILE, D. and FONDA, N. (1999) *Managing Learning for Added Value*. London, IPD.

6 SENGE P. M. (1990) *The Fifth Discipline: The art and practice of the learning organisation*. New York, Doubleday.

7 The following number of references to the term 'learning organisation' in books and articles were recorded by the CIPD Library for their catalogue purposes: 1996 − 38, 1997 − 28, 1998 − 50, 1999 − 33, 2000 − 23, 2001 − 13, and 2002 − 10.

8 Both quotations are taken from the ASTD's brochure on the 2003 Human Performance Improvement Certificate Program (see www.astd.org for fuller details). The definition of HPI is reproduced there and taken from ROTHWELL, W. (2002) *ASTD Models for Human Performance Improvement*, 2nd edition. Alexandria, Virginia, American Society for Training and Development.

9 SANDERS, E. S. (2002) 'What is HPI?' in PISKURICH, G. M. (ed.) *HPI Essentials*. Alexandria, Virginia, American Society for Training and Development.

10 JAMES, C. (2002) *Enterprise Talent Management: Need, opportunity, and challenges*, A Technical White Paper. Sun Microsystems, www.sun.com/2002-1008/feature/index.html.

3

What do we know about learning?

Listening skills could not be regarded as a key strength in the bank. Exercises based on effective (or active) listening were therefore built into most skills training events. Client handling skills for back office staff was just one example. The course had assembled and participants were divided into pairs. One of the pair was asked to pick a topic that mattered to him or her, and the partner was asked to listen without interruption but to indicate active interest using non-verbal signals. The first topic chosen by a participant was 'Why I think all training courses are a complete waste of time'.

The previous chapter concluded by presenting a set of factors that influence the effectiveness of learning in organisations. These factors, and others that will be developed later in the book, need to be taken into account if effective individual and team learning which promotes the organisation's objectives is to take place. The list of factors was about learning, not training. They were, however, constructed from the organisation's perspective, not the perspective of the individual learner. To that extent they were a top-down rather than bottom-up list. This chapter will offer a different viewpoint on the actions and interventions that might be taken to promote learning by considering how people learn in organisations.

As has been emphasised to date, moving the focus from training to learning requires a new mindset. Two illustrations may assist at this point. The first is light-hearted, and runs as follows. Ask any lecturer at one of our most traditional universities the following question, 'How do students learn at your university?' The guarantee is that within two sentences of the lecturer's answer the word *learn* will have been transposed to *teach* and he or she will proceed to describe the activities of lecturing, conducting tutorials and seminars.[1]

The second illustration shows how easy it is to fail to give due attention to some practical implications of the distinction between learning and teaching. It concerns the use of PowerPoint.

Learning PowerPoint

PowerPoint is a well-known Microsoft tool used in the preparation of presentations. It offers the user a range of options in presenting written text and non-verbal material. Many trainers make extensive use of the tool. In the spirit of the discussion in this chapter, some of these trainers were asked how they learned to use PowerPoint.[2]

During autumn 2002 data was collected from 102 individuals. They had attended five different presentations on e-learning: most were events organised by the Chartered Institute of Personnel and Development. The respondent population, therefore, were human resources professionals who were sufficiently motivated to attend seminars or conferences. Many of those attending would have been corporate training managers, some would have been full-time trainers and some training consultants. All respondents completed the questionnaire which is reproduced below.

Questionnaire used in research into the learning of Microsoft PowerPoint

1 How often do you use PowerPoint?

At least once a week ☐

More than once a month but not weekly ☐

Less than once a month ☐

Almost never ☐

2 How would you describe your level of expertise?

Experienced ☐

Adequate ☐

Struggling ☐

No expertise ☐

3 How did you gain your current level of expertise? (Please feel free to tick more than one)

Went on course lasting at least two hours ☐

Individual tuition by designated trainer ☐

Use of CBT/CD-ROM/Internet module ☐

Self-help plus advice from someone with more expertise ☐

Self-help plus use of Microsoft PowerPoint on-line help facility ☐

Self-help with none of the above ☐

Please comment on your learning (if you have ticked more than one we would like to know the sequence of methods)

----

4 What approach would you be most likely to use if you needed to extend your ability in Microsoft PowerPoint? (Please feel free to tick more than one)

Go on course lasting at least two hours ☐

Individual tuition by designated trainer ☐

Use of CBT/CD-ROM/Internet module ☐

Self-help plus advice from someone with more expertise ☐

Self-help plus use of Microsoft PowerPoint on-line help facility ☐

Self-help with none of the above ☐

Please add any comments

The first two questions seek to establish the frequency with which the respondent uses PowerPoint and his or her self-assessed level of expertise. The next two questions are multiple choice, where individuals identify learning methods that they have used or would use to acquire their capability.

Question 3 captures information on what may be described as current learning (how they reached where they are now). Question 4 captures information on intended learning – how respondents would be likely to acquire additional knowledge. The interpretation of Question 4 needs to be qualified: this does not, strictly speaking, reflect user preferences, simply what is likely to happen. For example, an individual could prefer to attend a course in future, but realistically recognises that one is not likely to be available.

These alternative methods can be classified into three groups, called for simplicity:

- structured: going on a course lasting at least two hours

- semi-structured: individual tuition by a designated trainer; use of CBT, CD-ROM, Internet module

- unstructured: self-help with or without advice from someone with more expertise and/or on-line help facility.

Since respondents are permitted to choose more than one option in Questions 3 and 4, up to 138 learning methods were indicated by the 102 respondents. These responses are summarised as Tables 3 and 4 below. Before these are discussed, some description of the population may be helpful.

As has been noted, the first two questions concern frequency of use and level of expertise. Question 1 collected information on frequency of use. There was a fairly even spread of responses here, with 'at least once a week' the most popular at 29 per cent. The second question asked for the self-addressed level of expertise: 25 per cent of respondents described themselves as experienced, 55 per cent adequate, 7 per cent struggling and 13 per cent no expertise.

The population could therefore be regarded as comprising a high proportion of regular users, and one with some confidence in its ability. How then did this relatively sophisticated population acquire its expertise, and how is it likely to acquire further expertise? Tables 3 and 4 offer some insights.

Table 3 | *How did you gain your current level of expertise?*

Went on course lasting at least two hours	27	structured	20%
Individual tuition by designated trainer	2	semi-structured	6%
Use of CBT/CD-ROM/Internet module	7		
Self-help plus advice from someone with more expertise	52	unstructured	74%
Self-help plus use of Microsoft PP on-line help facility	25		
Self-help with none of the above	5		
TOTAL	**138**		**100%**

Table 4 | **What approach would you be most likely to use if you needed to extend your ability in Microsoft PowerPoint?**

Go on course lasting at least two hours	26	*structured*	19%
Individual tuition by designated trainer	23	*semi-structured*	33%
Use of CBT/CD-ROM/Internet module	22		
Self-help plus advice from someone with more expertise	40	*unstructured*	48%
Self-help plus use of Microsoft PP on-line help facility	21		
Self-help with none of the above	5		
TOTAL	**137**		**100%**

The picture that emerges is clear. Three-quarters of the population acquired their current expertise by unstructured (self-help) methods. If they needed to extend their ability they would be most likely to continue to rely on these methods. However, the semi-structured options, individual tuition and the use of CD-ROM, which were not used to acquire current knowledge emerge as possibilities. The structured option, the formal course, attracted a fifth of responses for both current knowledge and as a way of extending expertise. Generally there seems to be satisfaction with what might be called self-directed learning.

This research is ongoing, and there is a danger of over-extending the analysis. As has been noted, there is a risk of confusing learning provision (what is possible) and learning preferences (what is desired). The former reflects what has been available to develop the acquisition of knowledge and skills, and the latter what might be available in future. The latter asks learners to choose between options, which may or may not be available.

Respondents were given the opportunity to offer comments. This data, taken it must be remembered predominantly from self-confident users (many of whom were trainers), contained some challenging observations. For example:

- 'A voyage of self-discovery', in many ways. More a case of "having a play" – sure I've missed some of the basics, but review and look.'
- 'Taught myself by trial and error – more advanced usage came when I had to teach others to use it and had to answer their questions! (At this point I had to access on-line help.)'
- 'I would not have the self-discipline to sit through an e-learning exercise. I usually only do something when I have to produce a result – I need to find out and be shown as quickly as possible, preferably by someone who knows how to do it!'
- 'A more structured approach may suit some people, but my preference is to have a go, and play with it!'
- 'I found this one of the most straightforward/intuitive packages to learn that I've come across.'
- 'Original course did not get put into practice. I went on course then did not access

PowerPoint for a week or more. So I forgot what I learned. I now book time to play when I return from IT training to ensure it sinks in.'

- 'Gap between course and using for work was too long. I forgot most of it.'

- 'No regular access to technology. Learning was for a one-off event. Neither practised nor integrated learning adequately.'

These comments, as can be seen, offer some insights on how individuals approach learning. The first five of the eight statements reveal something about the learner's preferences and experience. The latter three should remind trainers of something they know but may have neglected. Learning is different from training. There is no sense in sending people on a training event if they will not have the opportunity to practise their skills and knowledge. The timing of the event is therefore important and so, as the last statement poignantly reminds us, is access to equipment!

Learning in practice

Collecting information from learners on what they have learned, how they have learned it, and their preferences is quite different in concept and methodology from traditional top-down training needs analysis. It may be becoming more prevalent: there is some indication that learner-focused studies are being undertaken as e-learning is introduced. However, in general we simply do not know enough about how people learn.

Such surveys that have taken place, outside those concerned with e-learning, tend to draw on views from a wide variety of learners. The survey and research findings are often intended to inform the public policy debate. In 2002 the CIPD published the results of a telephone survey of 750 people who had received training at work in the preceding 12 months.[3] This showed that on-the-job training (defined in the survey as 'being shown how to do things, then practising them') was by far the most popular method of learning. Just over half of all respondents reported finding it the best method. A further 16 per cent rated 'learning from colleagues and people you work with' – an informal form of on-the-job training – their best method. Hardly anyone found on-the-job training and learning from colleagues the least appealing method of learning. A significantly higher proportion of women respondents (58 per cent) than men (42 per cent) said that being shown how to do things and practising them was their most popular learning method. Although classroom training comes equal second in popularity, only 16 per cent rated it their best way of learning, not far ahead of other methods.

Interventions which are focused on the learner (described earlier as learner-centred interventions) must take account of how people learn. This may appear self-evident, but can easily be overlooked in practice. There are both practical and theoretical issues to be considered. The PowerPoint example sheds light on some practical issues. Outlining the ways in which people acquired or felt they could acquire knowledge/skills revealed some important issues on learning design. In particular, the comments demonstrated the importance of timing if learning is to be transferred effectively to the job. One huge advantage of 'advice from someone with more expertise' is that it is likely to be delivered at the optimal time for the learning.

As in many of the issues raised throughout the analysis, to some extent we are returning to a previous debate. In 1953 Professor Robert James Havighurst, a Professor of Education at the University of Chicago, introduced the phrase 'teachable moments', which he described as follows (Havighurst, 1953[4]):

> *The tasks the individual must learn – the developmental tasks of life – are those things which constitute healthy and satisfactory growth in our society. They are the things a person must learn if he is to be judged and to judge himself to be a reasonably happy and successful person. A development task is a task which arises at or about a certain period in the life of the individual, successful achievement of which leads to his happiness and to success with later tasks, while failure leads to unhappiness in the individual, disapproval by the society, and difficulty with later tasks.*

(p.2)

> *When the body is ripe, and society requires, and the self is ready to achieve a certain task, the teachable moment has come. Efforts at teaching which would have been largely wasted if they had come earlier, give gratifying results when they come, at the teachable moment, when the task should be learned.*

(p.5)

Interestingly, the phrase 'teachable moment' (inevitably used without attribution) seems to be undergoing a resurgence. It is appearing at conferences over half a century later! This issue of appropriate timing of interventions will appear again in the course of this book.

Learning theories

In the remainder of this chapter the discussion will shift to a brief overview of learning theories. Much of this will be based on the Research Report prepared for the Chartered Institute of Personnel and Development by Cambridge Programme for Industry (CPI).

The Cambridge researchers were asked to review and synthesise the theories that govern our understanding of learning in organisations – and to express their results in a way that would be readily accessible to practitioners. An associated on-line learning site is available for open access at www.cipd.co.uk/howdopeoplelearn. The analysis presented in the CPI report will be supplemented by perspectives drawn from other commentators, particularly Dr Peter Honey, a leading UK commentator and writer on learning.[5] Three topics will be considered in turn: clusters of theories; learning and work; learning preferences and styles and learning to learn.

Theories by 'cluster'

The CPI Research Report suggested that the learning theories that have exerted most influence over the past 50 years could helpfully be placed into the following four clusters:[6]

- learning as behaviour
- learning as understanding
- learning as knowledge construction
- learning as social practice.

Immediately below is an edited summary of the analysis taken from the shorter 'Change Agenda' version of the CPI report.[7]

Learning as behaviour

The first cluster is concentrated around the theory of behaviourism and the work of B. F. Skinner. These theories originate from the natural sciences. Behaviourism asserts that any change in an individual's behaviour is the result of events, known as stimuli, and the consequences of these events. Reinforcing responses through reward is the behaviourist's way of encouraging the desired behaviours. By rewarding the desired behaviour the behaviourist conditions the individual to perform the action again and again.

Learning as understanding

Unlike behaviourism, which focuses on the conditioning of behaviour, cognitive learning theories view learning as a process of understanding and internalising the principles, connections and facts about the world around us. Seen this way, the learner is like a powerful machine that processes information and internalises it as knowledge.

Jean Piaget's notions of assimilation and accommodation offer an interesting perspective on how learning takes place. Assimilation refers to the integration of perceptions into existing mental models, whereas accommodation involves the alteration of mental models to explain perceptions that could otherwise not be understood. Equilibrium is achieved when a coherent mixture of strategies and rules can comfortably explain the world.

Strategies for cognitive development frequently deploy facilitation to assist understanding. By exposure to learning materials and guidance the learners can pass through developmental stages more quickly than if left to their own devices. Clearly, the facilitator needs to have a good understanding of where the learners are starting from in order to guide them effectively.

Learning as knowledge construction

Constructivist theories view the individual as an active agent in his or her own learning. Constructivists believe that all knowledge is personal knowledge – in other words, knowledge is not something 'out there' ready to be grasped. This means that knowledge is subjective, tacit and highly dependent on context. Constructivists would argue that knowledge management systems in fact manage information rather than knowledge, since the latter only exists inside people's heads.

Individuals assign meaning to knowledge that they have obtained through their own experience, and only then does it become usable. This focus on the learner contrasts with behaviourism where the 'expert' is the source of learning, or the cognitive approach where 'content' is emphasised. In constructivist theories the learner himself or herself is at the centre of the learning experience. Interaction and dialogue (with other learners or with a facilitator) are used by the learner to enhance his or her own personal experiences and understanding.

Learning as social practice

Social theories of learning do not contradict the behavioural, cognitive or constructivist theories.

Instead, they simply argue that learning is more effective when it arises and is applied in a social setting. This idea goes back to the work of L. S. Vygotsky who observed children interacting with older individuals. He discovered that they could perform well above their age if given the chance to interact with someone older. This led him to conclude that social interaction was crucial to some forms of learning.

Anthropologists, sociologists, social psychologists and cognitive theorists have all contributed to this cluster of theories. There are several different forms of social learning theories. Cognitive-social theories, as exemplified by Albert Bandura, regard learning as the outcome of social interactions which foster shared standards of behaviour. Activity theories regard established patterns of social interaction as the source of learning – for example, problem resolution within established work processes and patterns. Lastly, theories of social practice, made famous by Jean Lave and Etienne Wenger, point to the importance of participation in communities of practice as the source of learning. Here individuals don't so much learn facts and principles about the world as they learn, instead, how to 'be'.

No one learning theory is 'correct'. There is a continuing ongoing debate on their value.

For example, there seems to be a considerable interest at the time of writing in encouraging the creation of learning communities. These occur when groups of people consciously come together to learn from each other. In part this interest is a reflection of the new opportunities opened up by technology. This can be regarded as a reflection of a belief in the value of learning as social practice.

A sensible way of looking at these theories is to recognise that all of them can assist our thinking. All can help to clarify the steps that can be taken to assist learning and the learner. All have their place. It depends on the situation.

Equally, all can be badly or mis-applied. Sometimes organisations need to provide standardised information, often around product knowledge or systems change. The military is a good example. Learning and training have not often been the subject of poetry, but a famous exception is the poem by Henry Reed on the 'Lessons of the War'. In his opening section on the *Naming of Parts* he contrasts the tedious process involved in a class on the use of the rifle with activities outside the classroom.

Naming of Parts

Today we have naming of parts. Yesterday,
We had daily cleaning. And tomorrow morning,
We shall have what to do after firing. But today,
Today we have naming of the parts. Japonica
Glistens like coral in all the neighbouring gardens,
And today we have naming of parts.

The design of an effective process for learning involves far more than embracing a theory of learning (in this case learning as behaviour) and embedding it in a process of instruction. It is evident that the motivation of the learner and the environment in which people are expected to learn are critical influences on whether people learn. These will be considered in the third Part of the book.

Before leaving the theories of learning, one other comment should be offered. In as much as there is a dominant strand in thinking about effective learning in organisations today, it could be described as social-constructivism (or sometimes socio-constructivism) – an amalgam of the third and fourth categories. Learning is then a process of knowledge construction undertaken by the individual in a specific environment. The brief summary of learning activities in know-ledge-intensive firms that was presented at the beginning of Chapter 2 (see pages 19–20) can be seen to reflect a social-constructivist approach.

Learning and work

Cambridge Programme for Industry took these four clusters and used them to build up a 4 x 3 matrix incorporating their use *for, at* and *through* work. To reproduce the definitions used in the report[6] (p.15):

- For work: learning outside the workplace that is intended as preparatory or complementary to the work role ('just in case' learning). Typically conducted at the beginning of a career, it also spans learning activities throughout the working life. More broadly interpreted, learning for work occurs through contact with professional bodies, interest groups and external boards and committees of all kinds.

- At work: learning opportunities that are offered by the employer or as a consequence of employment, which require work to be set aside in favour of activities that stimulate or simulate (but do not replicate) work tasks.

- Through work: learning that occurs through direct work experience, individually or within teams or other collective groupings.

The resultant matrix (subsequently amended by CPI) is included as Table 5 and is offered, in the words of the report, 'to help reflect on the large number of ways that learning may be realised, and on the variety of resources and methods available to training and development practitioners'.

Since each theory has strengths and weaknesses, it is important to bear in mind the need to consider fitness-for-purpose when planning learning. The most positive outcomes are likely to occur when learning is linked directly to the job function, and opportunities are provided for immediate application of new-found capabilities.

Table 5 **| Summary of approaches to learning by cluster and focus**

	For work	At work	Through work
Behaviour	Priming	Instructor-led training	Guiding
Understanding	Engaging	Enriching	Problem-solving
Knowledge construction	Reflecting	Enquiring	Immersing
Social practice	Professional networking	Participation (in communities)	Teamworking

Source: Change Agenda *How Do People Learn?* prepared by Jennifer Schramm; p.28

Other factors also add another layer of complexity to the development of new approaches to learning. These include the climate for learning (including the physical environment) and the learners' motivation. It is increasingly recognised that individual motivation is of crucial importance. We will return to this topic in Chapter 7, pages 104–105.

Put simply, however, behavioural approaches are probably best suited to developing skills, cognitive approaches to increasing knowledge, constructivist approaches to enhancing performance, and socially mediated learning to accelerating change. In any particular situation, a mix of all four approaches might result in the best overall programme – richness of process is the key.

Learning preferences and styles

It is generally accepted that learners have different characters, strengths and preferences in the way they take in and process information. Given this, it is fair to argue that people will learn in different ways and one of the skills of the training professional is to adapt the approach to the individual.

In their report, CPI presented five or six commonly used classification systems, and these are reproduced as Table 6.

Table 6 | Learning style classification systems

Classification	Description
Myers–Briggs Type Indicator	This model classifies learners according to their preferences on scales derived from psychologist Carl Jung's theory of psychological types: extraverts or introverts; sensors or intuitors; thinkers or feelers; judgers or perceivers.
Felder–Silverman Learning Model	This classification has five categories – sensing or intuitive learners; visual or verbal learners; inductive or deductive learners; active or reflective learners; sequential or global learners.
Herrmann Brain Dominance Instrument	This method classifies learners in terms of their relative preferences for thinking in four different modes – left brain cerebral (logical thinkers) ; left brain limbic (sequential thinkers); right brain limbic (emotional thinkers); right brain cerebral (holistic thinkers).
Kolb's Learning Style Inventory	This classifies learners as having a preference for (a) concrete experience or abstract conceptualisation and (b) active experimentation or reflective observation.
Honey and Mumford's classification	Developed from Kolb's inventory and learning cycle, this model has four components – activists; reflectors; pragmatists; theorists.

Without doubt, the most successful model in the UK was that developed and popularised by Peter Honey and Alan Mumford. This drew, in part, from the work of David Kolb, an American academic and consultant.[8]

Kolb introduced the concept of the learning cycle: at stage 1 a person starts off with an experience; stage 2 of the cycle is to observe and reflect on that experience; stage 3 is to develop certain principles and concepts from that reflection; stage 4 is to test these principles and concepts either by replicating the initial experience or by trying out the principles in new circumstances. This will produce a new experience (stage 1 again), and the cycle continues. Some advocates of this approach would suggest that the individual's experience of the learning cycle could be paralleled by the organisation. In this case it is particularly important that the organisation ensures that there is adequate opportunity for stages 2 and 3 of the cycle (respectively called 'systematic reflection' and 'abstract conceptualisation') to take place.

Honey and Mumford's contribution was to postulate how a learning cycle could be used to identify learning styles. For them all the evidence suggested that individuals have learning styles. In the early 1980s they published a manual of learning styles that included a most useful and practical questionnaire; this was updated and reissued in 2000 (Mumford, 1999[9]; Honey and Mumford, 2000[10]).

Inevitably there are different issues on the substance and value of learning styles. A useful site is www.elsinnet.org.uk, which has been developed by an association of researchers, educationalists and trainers in ELSIN (the European Learning Styles Information Network). Generally there is acceptance that people develop preferences on how they learn. These are in place by the time they become adults, but it is open to debate whether they are innate or learned.

How this information in styles should influence the approach by the training professional can also be debated. On the one hand there is an argument that employers should become smarter in selecting the learning approach that suits the employee's preference. On the other hand there is an argument that to become really effective an individual can use a range of different approaches to learning: figuratively, they can then fire on all cylinders. As e-learning, in particular, advances in scope, this may become an increasingly important question. Should Ernst & Young, for example, deliver information to its geographically distributed workforce of auditors in a way that suits their preference (which must be effective in the short term)? Or should it try to develop their capabilities as rounded learners (which may be more effective in the long term)?

Such considerations link with the broader question of learning to learn. Peter Honey, as part of an ongoing project (as yet unpublished), defines it in the following terms:

Learning to learn is a process of discovery where you experiment with different approaches in order to:

- *increase your understanding of the principles of effective learning*

- *continuously improve your learning skills and expand your learning repertoire.*

So learning to learn is about both knowledge and skills. It is a subtly different concept from effective learning, but must also depend on an individual's behaviour. It is an important area that is ripe for future research.

Conclusion

Learning theory is a rich terrain and is continually developing. Much of the primary research has taken place in an educational, rather than an organisational context. Data is gathered from, or findings directed towards, schools, colleges or universities. This can make it hard for training professionals to see the relevance of the findings – and transfer is not always helped by mismatch between the vocabulary of the educational research and the language of the business place.

However, if the shift to learning from training is to be managed effectively, training professionals will need to gain a fuller understanding of how people can and do learn at work. Some of the more operational implications of what has been discussed in this chapter will be revisited in Part 3 of this book. There a discussion on the formulation and implementation of learner-centred interventions will be developed. First, however, the role of technology, and in particular e-learning, will be assessed. This will form the subject of the next two chapters.

REFERENCES AND READING

1 My appreciation to David Livesey, Secretary-General of the University of Cambridge for this illustration.
2 Much of the detailed analysis for this study was undertaken by Maram Al-Dowayan in the course of her studies at the University of Westminster.
3 CIPD (2002) *Who Learns at Work?* CIPD Survey Report. London, the CIPD.
4 HAVIGHURST, R. J. (1953) *Human Development and Education*. Chicago, David Mackay & Company; pp.2–5.
5 See www.peterhoney.com for details of his work. I am grateful to him for permission to reproduce his material.
6 REYNOLDS, J., CALEY, L. and MASON, R. (2002) *How Do People Learn?* Research Report produced by Cambridge Programme for Industry for the CIPD.
7 The quotations which describe the 'clusters' are taken from a summary Change Agenda *How Do People Learn?* CIPD (2002), prepared by Jennifer Schramm; pp.1–3.
8 KOLB, D. (1984) *Experimental Learning*. Englewood Cliffs, Prentice Hall.
9 MUMFORD, A. (1999) *Effective Learning*. London, Institute of Personnel and Development.
10 HONEY, P. and MUMFORD, A. (2000) *A Learning Styles Questionnaire* (80-item version). Peter Honey Learning.

Part 2

A new opportunity through technology

4

A progress report

Learning resource centres in the 1990s were designated rooms with PCs, libraries of computer-based training disks covering IT and soft skills, and books and videos. Use of the centre at the investment bank went into rapid decline after an initial launch. It was therefore encouraging to see a whole series of names from the back office team appearing in the signature book after a three-month gap. This group were normally not supporters of the training effort and it was felt best to leave them to get on with it rather than ask too many questions. Alas, a casual lunchtime inspection revealed that the learning resource centre had become the site of a regular card school.

This section of the book will offer a considered judgement of the contribution that e-learning (and blended learning) can make in shifting the focus to learning from training. What will these new technological developments mean for the paradigm of 'a focus on the learner'? This chapter considers progress so far: the next chapter will consider the potential of the new technology and what might be achieved.

The conclusion of this investigation is powerful. It was signalled in the Introduction. E-learning is a vital enabling mechanism: it will allow the focus on the learner to take place in a way that hitherto was not possible. However, if we are to move beyond aspirations towards implementation, it is essential that those involved in learning and training have the courage to make their views known. We must grasp the agenda.

Case studies are presented throughout this chapter and they will demonstrate that much has been achieved. Different types of e-learning will then be identified and analysed. The chapter will end with a consideration of the new emergence of blended learning. First, however, a brief overview of the circumstances that have led to the arrival of e-learning will be presented – what is it, and where has it come from?

The e-learning revolution

We have now experienced some four years of the e-learning revolution.[1] At the heart of what has happened is the connectivity of computers and the establishment of a network with protocols – a set of rules that govern the transmission of data. This network, the Internet, allows us to access up-to-date information anywhere at any time. All that is required is the initial information, a telephone line, a personal computer and a recipient learner.

Over this short period we have witnessed a peak of hope and a trough of cynicism resulting from a failure to deliver expectations. Initially e-learning was shamefully oversold. At the height of optimism the management guru, and author of *In Search of Excellence*, Tom Peters, addressed the Conference of the American Society for Training and Development (ASTD) held in Florida in June 2001. Urging his audience to progress more rapidly, he argued that the goal should be that 90 per cent of training in our organisations should be delivered electronically by 2003. A year later the problems of implementing e-learning had become apparent. The term 'blended learning' had emerged as a way of positioning e-learning in a more appropriate context. Suppliers had disappeared, merged, changed their names, and perceptions of e-learning were markedly different.

Given this turbulence it is understandable that there is a lack of consensus on the role of e-learning and how profound a change is taking place. Again it must be stressed that connectivity and Internet technology are new. Such uncertainty is reflected in the more general uncertainty about the power of the Internet as a business driver: this is illustrated by the summary that comprises the inset section below.

Summary

How has the Internet made a difference?

How much difference has the Internet made to the nature of competition, and how does this affect the place of learning? The more specific consideration of e-learning will be developed in the main body of this chapter. This inset section concentrates on the wider debate. As will be shown, the arguments offer some important insights on how we should view potential changes in the place of learning.

A useful starting point is to return to the work of Michael Porter and, in particular, his March 2001 *Harvard Business Review* article on 'Strategy and the Internet'.[2] As has been noted (in Chapter 1, p.5), Porter's central argument was that the basic rules covering strategy remain unchanged. However, the Internet had made a considerable impact in certain cases (p.66):

> *Its greatest impact has been to enable the reconfiguration of existing industries that had been constrained by high costs of communications, gathering information or accomplishing transactions. Distance learning, for example, has existed for decades, with about 1 million students enrolling in correspondence courses every year. The Internet has the potential to greatly expand distance learning, but did not create the industry.*

Porter recognised that the Internet will alter the relative importance of the forces that determine the competitive structure of industries. However, he did not see the Internet as representing a fundamental break from the past, but as the latest stage in the ongoing evolution of information technology.

Again, it is important to recognise the veracity of much of Porter's arguments. The People and Performance model considered in Chapter 1 (Figure 1) does not rely on the enhanced communication of the Internet. The central place of AMO (ability, motivation and opportunity), and the recognition of the expression of discretionary behaviour as a means of business advantage, do not depend on the transmission of information by means of networked computers.

There is, however, one important feature of the Internet that has a profound effect on business competition. It also has powerful implications on the place of learning and training in the modern organisation. This is because the Internet can change the relationship with customers. As the US commentator Don Tapscott, in a specific rejoinder to Michael Porter, put it (Tapscott, 2001[3]; p.40):

> *When it comes to customers, many pundits view the Net as simply another channel . . . But the Net is more than a channel. It changes all channels. Effective competitors equip sales agents with Net-based information and tools in the customers' living room. Call-center personnel with superior Net-based customer relationship management systems containing complete customer records deliver better customer service.*

In considering the relevance of this insight to learning and training we must begin by regarding the learner as a consumer. Moreover, the learner is an individual consumer with needs and preferences. The huge potential of the Internet arises from a changed relationship between the organisation and the individual. Connectivity allows the learning offering to be communicated directly to the individual. It changes the role of intermediaries including line managers and the training professional. Some consequences of this change will be introduced at later points throughout this book.

Definition and scope

There is as yet, no universally accepted definition of e-learning. On its website and in its surveys, the CIPD defines e-learning as 'learning that is delivered, enabled or mediated by electronic technology, for the explicit purpose of training in organisations'. This can be described as an inclusive definition: it includes the use of distributed technology products (mainly CD-ROMs) which do not require the user's computer to be networked. An exclusive definition would exclude these products and include only products delivered through the Internet or intranet.

If these distributed technology products are included, it could be argued that e-learning stretches back several decades. However, it is the emergence of the intranet that has offered far wider horizons, giving rise to whole new series of possibilities from connectivity – the process by which computers are networked and share information.

Once the positive features of this new medium for learning and training were recognised, a buzz of excitement was inevitable. These features remain: they have not disappeared because of subsequent problems that have emerged in implementation. The text box below contains a useful list developed by Stephenson in 2001.

At the outset it was recognised that e-learning could offer up-to-date information to learners who were widely distributed geographically. Collaboration and the sharing of information between learners would also be possible. Learners could generate their own material. However, if these were the advantages, there were also likely to be some challenges, problems and, indeed, drawbacks.

For example, learners would be likely to work in isolation. Some would enjoy it but for others it would be a profoundly unattractive and demotivating prospect. Some subject areas were clearly more suited to the new medium than others – it would be ideal for transferring hard information on, say, changes in tax structures but inappropriate for teaching feedback skills. Some learners

POSITIVE FEATURES OF E-LEARNING

Stephenson points to the following advantages of e-learning:

- ease of access to and interrogation of high volumes of diverse learning resources, including texts, pictures, library materials, learning tools and other aids to learning selected by the instructor

- ease of access to other materials from other sources, including non-educational sources

- ease of access to experts, inside and external to the institution

- interaction in various modes: teacher–student, student–student, student–learning materials

- interaction in various time dimensions: in real time (synchronous) or over a period (asynchronous)

- access to a range of personal support: by e-mail with tutor and mentors, or through peer group discussions

- ease of navigation to sources and persons within and outside the training course or materials

- logging or tracking of activities for personal records, sharing or assessment

- multiple levels of engagement to different depths of understanding, different volumes of data, difficulty of learning activities, according to individual capacity or interest

- feedback loops, either from teachers, peers and others or from within the materials themselves through progress checking, quizzes and online assessment

- links to other media, such as sound, video and TV

- ease of access to simulations of dangerous or complex activities for learning purposes

- choice of learning styles within the same package according to the needs of the learner

- global connectivity and collaboration opportunities

- flexibility of access from different locations.

Source: Stephenson (2001)[4]

were technophobic – and indeed so were some trainers. However, given its potential, the advance of e-learning was inevitable.

To date this advance has taken a number of different forms. Much of current experience is based on the use of web-based modules which are accessed at an individual's personal computer. In fact, as a learning tool, e-learning is much broader. In their report *How Do People Learn?*[5] Cambridge Programme for Industry produced the table which is reproduced (in an amended form) as Table 7. This identified three examples of current e-learning practice. Doubtless these will increase as new applications for learning through connectivity emerge.

Table 7 | E-learning: a typology

Web-based training	Supported on-line learning	Informal e-learning
Content is delivered to the learner without significant interaction or support from trainers, managers or other learners.	Learner interacts intensively with the tutor and other learners, supported by on-line content as appropriate.	Learner employs technology to communicate with colleagues and learn during the normal course of work.
From computer-based training	From open and distance learning	From knowledge management

To draw on the descriptions introduced in the Cambridge Programme for Industry Report:

Web-based training

In corporate training, technology is used primarily to deliver content to the end user without significant interaction with (or support from) training professionals, peers or managers. A significant industry has grown up around this form of e-learning, spanning content authoring, content asset management, instructional design and learning management. Key objectives of this form of e-learning are throughput and efficiency of development, management and delivery of content to learners.

Supported on-line learning

In higher education, the majority of the content of the course may be delivered through lectures or through distance-education textual material, but the course is categorised as e-learning because the interaction with the instructor, the dialogue with other students, the searching for resource materials, the conduct of collaborative activities, the access to course outlines and supporting material are all conducted on-line.

Informal e-learning

Beyond these 'course-based' approaches to e-learning are the growing opportunities for technology to support informal learning in the workplace. Informal learning is intimately related to job performance; it may not be formally organised into a programme or curriculum by the employer, but it accounts for a good deal of the learning arising out of interactions between colleagues, ad hoc personal studies, and the experience of work itself. In many knowledge intensive organisations it is linked with knowledge management (see Chapter 2, page 19–20, for definition).

Another classification has been articulated in a somewhat different form by the leading US commentator Allison Rossett of San Diego University. She used the terms *stuff* and *stir*. The *stuff* is the reusable web objects which are deployed on the corporate intranet. The *stir* refers to the collaborative tools of e-learning: the on-line discussions and virtual classroom.

Much has been achieved to date by organisations who are currently implementing e-learning. Accordingly, two case studies will be introduced at this stage. Ayrshire and Arran Primary Care National Health Service Trust illustrates the stuff (or web-based training, to use the classification set out in Table 7); the second from Ernst & Young illustrates the potential of the stir.

CASE STUDY

Ayrshire and Arran Primary Care National Health Service Trust

The Ayrshire and Arran Primary Care National Health Service Trust has redesigned its approach to the delivery of training on anaphylaxis. Its decision to produce a short web-based training module illustrates both the huge potential and real problems involved in this form of e-learning.

Ayrshire and Arran lies in southwest Scotland; it is geographically disparate, covering both the mainland and a series of offshore islands. The Trust employs some 1,100 qualified nurses, all of whom have direct contact with patients in the communities; many of them work independently and remotely. Anaphylaxis is a sudden allergic reaction following exposure to a substance to which a person proves sensitive (bee stings are just one example). Under extreme circumstances such a reaction can prove fatal. Prompt and appropriate diagnosis and action are essential. All of the Trust's nurses must therefore attend an annual training session on anaphylaxis and its treatment.

Traditionally such training was delivered through classroom sessions. However, the Trust's Training and Development Manager Ann Clark entered into discussions with Learning IT about a possible different approach. Learning IT is a Scottish IT training business based in Glasgow and Stirling whose main business is in delivery of face-to-face training, both for IT specialists and for end users. When Ayrshire and Arran explained their need, Learning IT developed an e-learning package of around an hour's duration. The course itself is hosted on the Learning IT website so learners simply log on to a given URL to access the course. This has the advantage that learners, wherever they are, are guaranteed to be taking the up-to-date version, and it also records learners who have completed the course.

The anaphylaxis module is the first web-based training to be produced for the Trust. The choice was deliberate. As Chris Rodden the Clinical Trainer puts it: 'Of all the training that I undertake, this one is the most information-intensive. Essentially it's stand-up instruction based on factual information which people must understand.' Clear learning objectives based on best practice can be specified for the training. The advantages of using the web for this form of knowledge-based training are evident. First, it is cheaper: a full cost analysis undertaken at the start indicated that the cost of an annual licence for this module would be more than outweighed by savings in travel, venue and trainer instruction time. Second, the module can be updated quickly if views on anaphylaxis treatment advance. Third, learners can learn at their own time and at a personal computer which is much nearer their place of work than the Trust's Headquarter Offices.

My thanks to Chris Rodden and Duncan Macleod for their assistance with the preparation of this case study.

CASE STUDY

Ernst & Young virtual classroom

Background
Most progress in e-learning has concerned web-based modules deployed on the corporate intranet (the 'stuff' of e-learning). The use of collaborative tools (the 'stir') has been much less prevalent in the corporate sector. Moreover, much of the use of collaborative tools has been through the

establishment of ongoing discussion groups. These groups have been asynchronous – learners can contribute and digest the contribution of others at any time to suit themselves.

A good example of the other type of collaborative tool – the virtual classroom – is the one used in the business and professional advisory firm Ernst & Young. 7,700 staff are employed by the firm across 22 UK offices delivering audit, tax and related business advice to private and public sector clients.

The model that is used by Ernst & Young is straightforward. A presentation typically of one hour in length is delivered over the intranet to individuals (or groups of individuals) who have pre-registered to access the material at their PCs. During the session the individuals hear a live audio commentary by dialling specific telephone numbers. They can ask questions either by telephone or by the preferred method of the chatroom function. Questions are displayed and answered on their screens. These can be seen by all participants. In this way an on-line discussion is established. Periodically during the session participants are asked interactive questions and offered a number of alternative answers – the results of this polling of participants are then displayed to all.

The topics chosen for such synchronous sessions are of importance to the organisation and the presentation is delivered and questions answered by a subject matter expert.

Progress to date
The technology platform used was developed in the late 1990s by the US Ernst & Young practice. The first use of the virtual classroom took place in the UK in January 2001 when some 100 staff participated in a pilot session. The subject chosen was 'e-immersion': this outlined the firm's view on how the Internet-related products that it would offer its clients could develop.

The session was hosted from the United States, and this remains the practice. To the learner the only issue that this raises is the speed of access and response to questions. It has to be said, however, that maintaining the robustness of the technology platform has been a major area of concern to the UK training team.

Since that initial pilot the virtual classroom approach has been used for a growing number of sessions. In the year 2002 some 37 sessions were held in which around 3,800 members of staff participated.

Important virtual classroom sessions included:

- updates for all audit staff on the methodology which Ernst & Young use across the world
- an introduction to the career counselling process
- an introduction to the new learning management system which Ernst & Young has rolled out – this has been the biggest session to date, with over 400 'counselling managers' participating
- a session involving 30 of the most senior staff who were participating in an Account Leaders' Development Programme (a senior management development initiative) – this was designed to

CASE STUDY continued

allow them to share information in their development progress to date, and the presentation was delivered by one of the most senior partners in the firm

- an update in the 2002 Finance Bill presented by the Head of National Tax
- a presentation by the new National Tax Partner in his vision for the future and goals of the UK tax practice. Three sessions were held on the future of the tax practice and each involved over 200 participants. They were delivered to groups of tax professionals assembled in meeting rooms or classrooms
- a session available to the global team serving GE Capital, an important Ernst & Young client. Some twenty staff participated from around the world.

Feedback on the Ernst & Young virtual classroom can be obtained from an end-of-session polling screen. This asks: was the learning effective, how was the technology, and would you recommend this approach to other users? User Statistics (number of participants and time of session) are also collated. However, participants are also asked for their end-of-session comments, and these are in many ways the best guide to further progress.

Some issues
The Ernst & Young learning and development team have not found it necessary to promote the virtual classroom. Its growth has been a product of the effectiveness and acceptance – it has spread through 'viral marketing' or word of mouth. In the view of Brenton Hague, the Senior Learning and Development Manager responsible for initiative, the long-term pattern in the UK could involve some 10 virtual classroom presentations a month across the firm. Each would involve some 70 participants who would be more experienced and senior professionals.

So why has it worked? First, it can be seen that the sessions concerned the transmission or dissemination of up-to-date hard information of value to the participants in their work. This has ranged from technical information (tax and audit) through to information (but not skills practice) required for the staff development process. The relevance of the one client-oriented session (for GE Capital described above) is a powerful illustration of a pattern that could be of considerable importance in the future. According to Brenton Hague, 'In many ways it's a communication tool as much as a learning tool. It is powerful when there is a need to get a message to lots of people in a short time. It's about good, up-to-date information from experts being transferred quickly.' Reflecting this characteristic there is some discussion within Ernst & Young as to whether the approach should be described as a virtual classroom or virtual presentation. The former term implies a more participative approach. However, the only sensible conclusion is that what it is called, and how it is categorised, does not matter. It is effective in improving performance and therefore valued by the organisation.

The spread of the virtual classroom in Ernst & Young has undoubtedly been assisted by two characteristics of the firm. First, there is a sophistication in the use of technology and universal availability of access to PCs. Second, and perhaps crucial, there is a general acceptance of the importance of knowledge to the business: this is what Ernst & Young does – it puts expert knowledge to use in the interests of its clients. There is therefore a positive attitude to learning in an environment where time pressures are considerable. These factors mean that the transfer of this approach elsewhere may be much more challenging.

My thanks to Brenton Hague and Sue Westwood for their assistance with the preparation of this case study.

However, the potential of e-learning has extended way beyond the public and corporate sector. The explosive growth of the Internet as a leisure as well as a business tool has led the enthusiasts to create a multiplicity of sites. Many of them are impressive repositories of information which provide opportunities for learning through collaborative activity even though this is not their primary intention. The Clan Macpherson site (www.clanmacpherson.org) not only contains a wealth of information in the history of the clan, but offers an uplifting rendition of *Flower of Scotland*. By contrast, the Welsh Rugby Nation site (www.icwales.icnetwork.co.uk/0500rugbyunion) addresses the other end of the emotional scale: it offers the despondent supporter some emotional therapy through sharing opinions on the causes of the tragic national demise.

A particularly interesting community learning site is TriggerStreet.com (www.triggerstreet.com). This was created, developed and launched by Dana Brunetti, and is supported by the Hollywood actor Kevin Spacey. It aims to give novice film-makers a forum where their work can be seen online and be discussed and reviewed by peers. It describes itself as a community of reviewers and creators. Some traditional approaches to informal learning continue as before: the Sharrington Village Ladies Reading Group, in North Norfolk, meets once a month to discuss a novel of choice and does not operate a site.

Progress to date

Given such impressive initiatives, and the undoubted long-term potential of e-learning, progress to date must be regarded as a disappointment. Significant training surveys from both sides of the Atlantic underline the extent of the problem.

Every year the American Society for Training and Development (ASTD) publishes a survey based on responses obtained from its benchmark forum of corporate and public sector organisations.[6] Respondents are asked to estimate the current percentage of training delivered by learning technology and the percentage that they expect to be delivered in three years' time. Responses to the first question have been as follows: 9.1 per cent in 1997; 8.5 per cent in 1998; 8.4 per cent in 1999; 8.8 per cent in 2000; 10.5 per cent in 2001 (this last is the latest figure available as there is an inevitable reporting time-lag). The 'three years forward' estimate has consistently been more than double these figures. For example, the 2001 'actual' of 10.5 per cent was collected at the same time as a projection of 25.0 per cent for 2004. There is evident optimism here: all problems will be overcome and success is but three years away. Welsh rugby supporters will recognise this mindset: we have adopted it for the last ten seasons.

At the same time, the results of the 2002 CIPD annual survey of training managers were published. It also showed no evidence of an e-learning explosion in the UK. Only 30.5 per cent of the 500 UK training managers surveyed had introduced e-learning, and of those almost three-quarters describe their use as 'a little'. By the following year the figure had increased to just under half: 47.8 per cent of respondent training managers had introduced e-learning. There was a particularly marked increased in the availability of e-learning for manual staff.

However, over the four years of e-learning there have been expressions of interest in many different approaches, but the main growth area for e-learning to date has been in web-based products ('the stuff'). These have been highly promoted; almost all of the promotion has concentrated on the potential cost savings using these modules. This may have acted to the long-term detriment of the growth of e-learning.

Those who attended training exhibitions on conferences could well have received a letter from a supplier of e-learning containing the following questions (or similar sentiments):

- Not able to take time out from your job to attend a traditional classroom-based course?

- Is your team geographically spread across a number of locations, countries, or not available to attend a traditional-based course as a group?

- Is your training budget a little squeezed at the moment and you cannot afford the travel and accommodation costs associated with traditional courses?

Training managers who answered yes to any of the above questions were invited to contact the vendor for 'an alternative solution'. It would be hard to envisage a training manager who would not be able to answer yes to at least one of the three! True, an increasing number of organisations are achieving real efficiencies, reflected in cost savings. These are mainly organisations where there is a need to provide standardised information, often around systems change, to a large workforce with a geographical spread, and where members of this workforce already have IT skills.

In the course of the 2002 CIPD survey the one-third of training managers who had introduced e-learning were presented with a number of statements about e-learning. They were asked whether they strongly agreed, agreed, disagreed or strongly disagreed with the statements. The four statements that secured the most agreement are reproduced below:

- E-learning demands a new attitude to learning on the part of the learners.

- The first generation of e-learning products does not demonstrate what the future will look like.

- E-learning demands an entirely new skills set for people involved in training and development.

- E-learning is more effective when combined with more traditional forms of learning.

What this succinctly emphasises is a disparity of perspectives. In the first years of e-learning vendors sold products on the basis of cost savings; training managers had recognised that a huge change management process was required.

Blended learning

Blended learning can be seen as part of a response to the failure to date of e-learning to achieve potential. Such cynicism aside, it is important to ask a number of questions and consider what is meant by this term, how much it is new, and how much substance there is in the term. Human resource development loves to embrace a concept in search of an application. Is there real meaning behind the term 'blended learning', and if so, what?

Blended learning, as the term is used today, is an approach to training design that involves the use of a combination of delivery methods and in some cases learning methodology. Since it first appeared in 2001 the term has achieved considerable momentum. It has been used as a convenient peg for conferences and as a title in innumerable articles. To an extent its emergence must be seen as a reaction to the undiscriminating and unsupported offer of web-based learning modules. Blended learning suggests that e-learning will be most effective when it is part of an overall strategy involving the classroom and on-the-job workplace learning. This is an intuitively attractive proposition, but hardly new.

The idea of combining different methods of instruction has a long history. Readers may recall the following extract from Charles Dickens's *Nicholas Nickleby*. Mr Squeers, the proprietor of the Dotheboys Hall School, seems to be prepared to vary his approach to take account of different learning styles. He demonstrated his approach to education to his new employee, Nickleby, in the following manner. Was he ahead of his time in recognising the value of blended learning?

'Now then, where's the first boy?'

'Please, sir, he's cleaning the back parlour window,' said the temporary head of the philosophical class.

'So he is, to be sure,' rejoined Squeers. 'We go upon the practical mode of teaching, Nickleby; the regular education system. C-l-e-a-n, clean, verb active, to make bright, to scour. W-i-n, win, d-e-r, der, winder, a casement. When the boy knows this out of the book, he goes and does it. It's just the same principle as the use of the globes. Where's the second boy?'

'Please, sir, he's weeding the garden,' replied a small voice.

'To be sure,' said Squeers, by no means disconcerted. 'So he is. B-o-t, bot, t-i-n, tin, bottin n-e-y, ney, bottinney, noun substantive, a knowledge of plants. When he has learned that bottinney means a knowledge of plant, he goes and knows 'em. That's our system, Nickleby; what do you think of it?'

However, in its modern manifestation, when technology is available to enhance the mix, blended learning becomes an attractive approach. An example will demonstrate its worth. It concerns the development of business advisers in Scotland and is presented as the case study below.[8]

CASE STUDY

The Scottish Enterprise Premier Adviser programme

Overview

Premier Adviser is a programme for business advisers aimed at enhancing their capability in providing guidance to clients, mainly in developing businesses in Scotland. There are 800 eligible business advisers based in Scotland: the majority work for Scottish Enterprise, who devised and manage the programme; others are employed by Enterprise Trusts and local authorities, or operate as independent consultants. The programme is currently being developed and extended to advisers who work for Scottish Enterprise in overseas locations – but the immediate concern is the quality of provision in Scotland. Here, in June 2000, a Scottish Parliament report identified an urgent need 'for better professional training of business advisers, and the development of a formal accreditation system'.

A programme was devised and a pilot group of 45 advisers commenced their studies in autumn 2000. The success of the pilot led to the accelerated introduction of a full programme in July 2001.

The first groups have now completed the programme and have received accreditation. At the time of writing, advisers are participating at differing stages in the programme. A new group of 20–25 advisers joins every fortnight, and it is intended that all 800 advisers identified will complete in due course. A lower-level programme for those who offer Business Information is shortly to be introduced.

Programme design
The programme has a number of co-ordinated elements; some are designed to assist advisers in identifying and acquiring necessary skills; some provide the opportunity to demonstrate their knowledge.

The year-long programme starts with a one-day launch workshop for the group of 24 participants. As well as a general programme outline, participants are introduced to the on-line learning modules and allocated a mentor. They must then produce their own Continuous Personal Development (CPD) plan. This is created using an on-line self-assessment tool, which helps the participant identify, in co-operation with others, their strengths and weaknesses. They then must allocate 60 hours spread across the year to activities which will develop strengths and overcome weaknesses. Regular monthly reports on progress must be forwarded using an on-line template.

The following learning opportunities are available over the year:

- support from a mentor to assist with any difficulties on on-line loan access, advise on the CPD plan and accompany participants on case study visits
- access to 72 hours of on-line learning material covering a variety of topics including finance, marketing and human resources. A local specialised e-learning company, The Knowledge Business, produced the on-line learning site. There are support materials which have been sourced from various providers or written specifically for the programme facilities and chat rooms associated with the on-line provision of material. Satisfactory completion of module tests is required of the learners
- attendance at workshops. Here the cohort is brought together for a one-day session to discuss case-based material on business advice. There are four separate workshops held over the year. At the end of each, participants are required to complete an assessment which is submitted on-line

- participation in less formal monthly action learning groups held with other group members
- identification of case study client organisations (generally participants will choose two, though this depends on the nature of their role). Over a year guided by their mentor, participants are expected to offer evidence of the efficiency of their interventions. They must demonstrate that their input achieved clear outputs, which worked to the benefit of their client organisations.

Assessment and accreditation

At the end of the year, when all activities have been completed, participants are assessed at a panel interview. Learners need to present their monthly progress logs, and assignment and case study material. Successful candidates are awarded an accredited Diploma in Business Counselling, which, under the Scottish Credit Accumulation Transfer System, counts as a third of a Master's Business degree.

Where candidates are experiencing difficulty in achieving the standard, additional support or time is allowed to enable them to work toward meeting the standard. Every effort is made to adjust timescales to meet candidate needs, but all advisers must reach the standard by September 2003.

Some issues

This is evidently a successful, well-constructed programme, which achieves a clearly defined need. It is important to identify some of the factors that have led to its success before taking any position on its transferability to other situations.

First, there was a compelling case for its introduction: acceptance by key parties of the Scottish Parliament's recommendation led to powerful support. This is reflected in the resources committed to an impressive, multi-faceted design for learning, which involves classroom, on-line, action learning, self-directed learning and mentoring. The Scottish Enterprise estimates the programme cost approximately £2.2 million.

The one area where support has been less than universal is the learner population themselves. As Bill McGrath, the Head of Network Development at Scottish Enterprise who devised and managed the programme, puts it, 'We face the problems of dealing with an installed base of advisers. Some (including those who volunteered for the pilot) see a lot of value in enhancing their capability through learning; others don't see the point and will resist.'

Particular resistance can apply to what is for some the novel format of on-line learning. Here Bill McGrath argues that the vast majority are agnostics, and quite often at four months there is a sea change in those who are hostile.

My thanks to Bill McGrath for his assistance with the preparation of this case study.

Against such undoubted success stories, what are we to make of the term 'blended learning'? First let us examine the way the term is commonly used. The unfortunate conclusion is that blended learning is somewhat of a misnomer, being used to describe blended training. There is a big difference. To return to the definitions used in *How do People Learn?*[5] and cited in the Introduction:

> *Learning is the process by which a person constructs new knowledge skills and capabilities: whereas training is one of several responses of responsibilities an organisation can undertake to promote learning.*

To date, the 'blend' discussion has concentrated almost entirely on what the trainer should do to make an intervention effective (blended training), not on getting the appropriate mixture to meet the needs of the recipient (blended learning). Discussion is focused on the combination of delivery methods, not the response of the learner.

Blended learning, defined in this way, is by no means a new concept. Consider the following quotation taken from a work of Robert Gagne,[9] arguably the most influential figure in the development of instructional design:

> *Although practical considerations are often involved, selection of media for instruction is ideally based upon the characteristics of the medium and its predicted success in providing appropriate conditions for the learning of each kind of intended learning outcome.*

Over his lifetime Gagne produced a series of works in which the principles of effective design were clarified and codified. Other commentators, particularly in the USA, extended the analysis as new means of training delivering became available. The idea underlying 'blended learning' has been there for several decades. What is new is the enhanced opportunities for its implementation.

So is blended learning simply effective instructional design? The answer, at this stage, is probably yes – but this is in no way denigrating the efforts of the training managers who are demonstrating best practice. Such solutions are likely to be more effective than a design based on a single delivery approach, but at an inevitable cost. So how should we feel about the term 'blended learning'? Should we welcome it or discourage its use as an example of old wine in new bottles?

In practice this question is becoming increasingly academic. Blended learning has arrived as a term: suppliers of e-learning systems and organisers of conferences are giving it huge momentum. We must try to give it coherent meaning rather than allowing it to be yet another round of hype that has surrounded the development of e-learning. This will be achieved by concentrating on the implications for learning and the learner.

More importantly, in one respect, the arrival of the term may well prove to be beneficial. One participant at a recent conference made a powerful point, and I am grateful to her for drawing it to my attention.[10] Her argument was that some managers may be suspicious of e-learning. The term 'blended learning' however describes and allows a useful dialogue on the elements of the 'blend' to take place. In particular, it allows the trainer to emphasise the importance of effective involvement of line managers.

REFERENCES AND READING

1   The earliest article on the emerging new concept in a journal held in the CIPD Library dates from 1995: SUNOO, B. P. (1995) 'America Online boosts up for hypergrowth', *Personnel Journal*, Vol 74, No. 12, December; pp.28–37. It describes how America Online (AOL) was 'establishing an electronic information service to converge online, multimedia and the Internet'. This required AOL to 'develop special HR strategies for training, culture creation and operator support'. The article did not use the term 'e-learning'. This term first appeared in the writings of the US guru Elliott Masie towards the end of 1999. In the following year it began its explosive growth as a subject for discussion and analysis.

2   PORTER, M. E. (2001) 'Strategy and the Internet', *Harvard Business Review,* March; pp.63–77.

3   TAPSCOTT, D. (2001) 'Rethinking strategy in a Networked world (or why Michael Porter is wrong about the Internet)', *Strategy & Business*, Issue 24, 3rd Quarter; pp.37–41.

4   Adapted from STEPHENSON, J. (2001) 'Learner-managed learning – an emerging pedagogy for learning online', in J. Stephenson (ed.) *Teaching and Learning Online*. London, Kogan Page; p.220.

5   REYNOLDS, J., CALEY, L. and MASON, R. (2002) *How Do People Learn?* Research Report produced by Cambridge Programme for Industry for the CIPD.

6   THOMPSON, C., KOON, E., WOODWELL, W. H. and BEAUVAIS, J. (2002) *Training for the Next Economy*. Alexandria, Virginia, the American Society for Training and Development (www.astd.org).

7   CIPD Training and Development 2002 Survey Report (London, CIPD) and CIPD Training and Development 2003 Survey. London, the CIPD.

8   The case study previously appeared in an article 'Making sense of blended learning', *Training Journal*, October 2002, pp.12–15, and is reproduced with thanks.

9   GAGNE, R. and MEDSKER, K. L. (1996) *The Conditions of Learning: Training applications*. Texas, Harcourt Brace; p.180.

10 I am indebted to Ann Jakeman for this insight.

5

Potential and reality

Some managers in investment banking were sympathetic to the role of training but simply did not have the experience or skills to operate effectively. One individual who fell into this category was a highly respected trader who was given a new task: he was asked to chair the training committee, covering the group of corporate stockbrokers, dealers and investment analysts. He asked me for guidance. I recommended that our work started with a questionnaire inviting all staff to indicate the training they had received to date, their development aspirations and their training needs. Once this stage had been completed I reported back to the first meeting of the committee that some useful results had been assembled and all but five employees had completed the questionnaire. The Chair then demanded the names of the five who had failed to comply with the request. On discovering that one was an immediate subordinate he rushed out to the trading floor and frog-marched the unfortunate young man into the meeting room. 'Right, you *** ! Fill the *** form in NOW!' he said. We all watched horrified as the recalcitrant individual was publicly made to write his answers to questions like 'What are your main ambitions for the next three years?' and 'How can training assist you in your job?'

The previous chapter considered the emergence of e-learning – and the later arrival of blended learning. What has happened is of huge importance. Connectivity, the ability to make updated information available over a telephone line to anyone with a PC, creates a whole range of new possibilities for learning and training. Progress to date may have been patchy, but the potential is immense.

Some human resource professionals have appeared slow to grasp the importance of this new agenda. Indeed, some have appeared wary, even frightened by the new technology. To them the evidence of mounting problems with e-learning is greeted with *Schadenfreude* (a malicious pleasure in the misfortune of others) – and a cry of 'I told you so!' Such attitudes and actions are mistaken and must be resisted. They fail to take account of lessons from history. The full potential of any new technology takes time to be realised; we must expect some false starts. There are always early misunderstandings on what the technology can achieve.

A good example is offered by the railway age in the UK – generally accepted as a defining period in the first Industrial Revolution. When railways arrived they were seen as a serious competitor to the canals for the transport of heavy goods between industrial centres. Doubtless there was much chatter on the towpaths among canal operators reassuring each other that this new fad would pass. Such sceptics would have been considerably reassured by the events of 1845. In that year a huge speculation in railway shares was followed by a spectacular crash even in the shares of the companies that became giants of the industry. Nothing new in the roller-coaster of dot.com shares.

The railways survived and the canals declined. What is instructive is the diverse impact of the railways. In giving ordinary people access to the coast, for example, the railway created the modern British seaside and transformed leisure. Here's an interesting fact: before the arrival of the railway network, time across British towns and cities varied. The time in Gloucester was different from the time in Oxford. However, in order to ensure predictable times for departure and arrival, national times were introduced as a consequence.

Sometimes major developments can emerge in some quite unexpected ways.

A recent and more relevant example concerns the development of e-mail. In an accessible book on the origins of the Internet, the academic and journalist John Naughton describes how e-mail emerged from the work of the Advanced Research Projects Agency (ARPA). The following quote (Naughton, 2001[1]; p.141) speaks for itself.

> *E-mail came as something of a surprise to ARPA – or at least to some people in it. The Net was funded, remember, to enable the research community to share scarce resources. The idea was that the researchers at a site would be able to log into – and run – programmes on computers at other sites. So imagine ARPA's puzzlement when a specially commissioned survey in 1973 revealed that three-quarters of all the traffic on the Net was electronic mail. . . . Worse still, some of these messages were not even about computing!*

There is every possibility that new opportunities will arise as a result of the technology, which can make learner-focus a reality. One key fact lies behind this claim: technology (and the networked PC in particular) alters the interface between the organisation and the individual; it allows the individual and the organisation to relate to each other in new and exciting ways.[2] As a result, new developments can be envisaged which could radically improve learning in organisations. Some of these are already taking place; some are at an embryonic stage; some are still no more than feasible ideas.

Three will be considered in this chapter. They are: first, a blurring of boundaries; second, time and speed to market; third, personalisation or the market of one. Together, these developments raise a fundamental question – does e-learning offer a different model of learning? This question will be explicitly considered in the concluding section of this chapter. First, however, it should be recognised that the product or service range offered by e-learning vendors is likely to change. Figure 5 is followed by a short analysis.

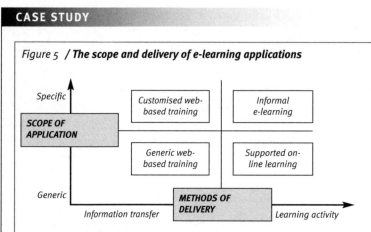

Figure 5 / *The scope and delivery of e-learning applications*

My thanks to Jake Reynolds for his assistance in the preparation of this Figure.

Explanation of the terms in the quadrants of Figure 5

Generic web-based training (descended from computer-based training): where content is delivered to the learner without significant interaction or support from trainers, managers or other learners.

Customised web-based training: as generic web-based training in application, but designed to achieve a very specific learning objective – often produced using in-house authoring tools.

Supported on-line learning: where the learner interacts intensively with a tutor and other learners, supported by content as appropriate.

Informal e-learning: where the learner employs technology to communicate and learn with colleagues during the normal course of work.

Results from the CIPD Training and Development Survey 2002[3] indicated powerfully that training managers recognised the limitations of the first generation of e-learning products (see Chapter 4, pp.55–6). General content available at that time reflected what had previously been available on CD-ROM (and before that, CBT disk) and fell mainly into one of the following categories:

- information technology for end users (for example, Microsoft products)
- information technology for IT specialists (for example, HTML or Java script)
- data relating to management and interpersonal skills (for example, coaching, leadership, project management).

The first two gained the most acceptance. However, all three fell into the category of web-based material and as such represented only part of the potential contribution of technology to learning and training. Figure 5 above is an attempt to categorise e-learning applications in two respects. The vertical axis considers the scope. (Is it very specific to the user or much wider in its application?) The horizontal axis looks at how it is delivered, distinguishing between the transfer of information and ongoing learning activity.

CASE STUDY continued

The early applications of e-learning have been firmly in the bottom left-hand corner: they are concerned with the transfer of generic information. There are limits to the growth potential in this quadrant. Much current activity is taking place in the top left-hand corner (customised web-based training) and there is a growing recognition of the potential of supported on-line learning in the corporate context. In general in the future there will be a migration of e-learning from this bottom left quadrant, and this will create new opportunities in the organisational context.

Blurring the boundaries

This is the first of the three developments which could radically alter our view of e-learning.

It is easiest to explain in terms of an illustration. Consider the example set out in the case study in the previous chapter which described how Ayrshire and Arran Primary Care National Health Service Trust had, for entirely laudable reasons, developed a web-based training model to out-line the treatment of anaphylaxis.

The power of the underlying approach is evident. If this learning module proves effective, it is capable of wide extension. Anaphylaxis is the same throughout the country, and, presumably,

CASE STUDY

The International Virtual Medical School (www.ivimeds.org)

As societies demand ever-improving health care, so time pressures on medical training increase. An attractive approach is to solve what is an increasingly global problem through cross-border collaboration, using e-learning techniques. It is this perspective that has led to the creation of the International Virtual Medical School (IVIMEDS) project. Over 50 medical schools were represented at founding discussions hosted by the Centre for Medical Education, University of Dundee, in June 2002.

The Dundee Centre has a tradition of delivering medical education, at a variety of levels, through distance learning techniques. It has developed competency-based approaches and has placed considerable emphasis on the need for training to lead to clear learning outcomes. Much medical delivery involves a mixture of knowledge, skills and judgement. For a doctor, for example, the Dundee Centre has put forward a mixture of capabilities based on what the doctor has to do, the approach to doing it, and the need for professionalism throughout all engagements.

The Dundee Centre's interests range from the training of student doctors to graduate level, their subsequent continuous professional development, a variety of diplomas and updating courses for other clinical staff, and a Master's programme in medical education for health care professionals. The Centre has developed a particular expertise in judgement-based assessment tools (which have also been produced for the police on a contract basis), in curriculum planning, and in the general topic of how people learn medical knowledge and skills. Traditionally, much of the Centre's distance learning output has been print-based, although it has produced scenarios involving video clips and question and information options. These are seen as useful tools in problem-based learning.

The University of Dundee Centre for Medical Education was the driving force behind the IVIMEDS initiative and had the support of all the Scottish medical schools. Other prominent sponsors were the University of Miami (which has considerable experience in the production of e-learning material), the University of Queensland, and a consortium of Catalonian schools centred on Barcelona.

All medical schools throughout the world face similar problems. Resources are stretched as student numbers expand and the curriculum is extended as medical knowledge increases. The IVIMEDS launch brochure suggests that medical schools are faced with a number of challenges and that collaboration using e-learning must form part of the response. These challenges are identified as: transforming how students learn; sharing expertise and resources; delivering a high-quality and financially sustainable programme; increasing access to medical education (this challenge has immense implications for the assistance of less developed countries); working in partnership with continuing education; providing leadership in medical education.

The argument is that the technology is now available to allow medical schools across the world to share resources. It is financially beneficial to all parties to share teaching materials; and participation in IVIMEDS will give them access to a rich pool of ready information.

Immediately the initiative is concentrating on accumulating and cataloguing (or tagging) distance learning resources on two main subjects of medical importance: hypertension and the treatment of strokes. Over 250 such 'reusable learning objects' (to use the term adopted by IVIMEDS to describe any self-contained item which can assist learning) have been identified to date. They consist of text objects, video clips and some more sophisticated scenario-based modules which allow interactive learner participation.

In addition to the bank of reusable learning objects, another priority for the initial phase of IVIMEDS is the development of curriculum maps for the training of doctors. The systematic structuring of material needed to support such a curriculum is an increasingly complex and demanding activity. It is another area where collaboration across international boundaries could produce real results and economies of effort.

The IVIMEDS vision was sufficiently compelling to bring over 50 schools to an initial conference where the initial proposal was outlined. Stage 2 is a full feasibility study that commenced in February 2003 and is due to be completed a year later. In the course of Stage 2 participant schools will not only contribute learning material in the form of reusable learning objects but also make a financial commitment and actively participate in the development of all aspects of IVIMEDS. A number of organisational models are under consideration: some are based on extensive teaching on an agreed IVIMEDS curriculum; others will encourage shared resources but allow greater local autonomy on teaching and assessment.

CASE STUDY continued

Professor Ronald Harden, formerly the Director of the Centre for Medical Education and now Director of Education for IVIMEDS, who provided much of the early impetus for the project, sees the challenge in the following terms:

The scale of the exercise – with over 50 participant schools – presents problems in itself. There is a need to secure a consensus and alignment on objectives which are far from straightforward. At the same time we need to demystify the e-learning component: some schools have a high awareness, some none.

The IVIMEDS initiative is visionary and deserves to succeed. There is a tradition of medical co-operation which will assist. Prestige and status of the participant schools will be enhanced by the initiative. The danger to progress may be a 'not invented here' reaction to the shared material and a reluctance to change instructional patterns in the constituent departments in the schools. IVIMEDS is a change management project as much as it is a teaching initiative.

My thanks to Professor Ronald Harden and Dr Natalie Lafferty for their assistance with the preparation of this case study.

the world. If an effective and successful module is produced, why should anyone else produce another? Similarly, if the principles underlying the training module prove effective, the same approach can be adopted for other essential clinical training. The compelling vision behind this idea has been recognition as the basis for the International Virtual Medical School case study.

This case study demonstrates the potential in collaborative approaches. Communities can produce material which is designed specifically for their needs and then share the content with others. E-learning has the potential to flow across (or blur) organisational boundaries. Different groups within different organisations (and in the IVIMEDs case, different countries) can work with each other because this is their preference. This has been a feature of behaviour in a profession for some time. The new technology makes it much easier (and difficult for the restrictive organisation to prevent!).

Blurring of a different form can also take place: categories of intervention can blur into one. Take the example of the anaphylaxis web-based module. If it is used for training purposes, it is a learning module; if it is placed on a repository at the IVIMEDs (see the case study above), it becomes knowledge management. Suppose, in the age of the super mobile technology that we are told will arrive, the same module is made available to someone who is about to treat a patient with suspected anaphylactic shock. It then becomes a performance support. Which is it? Two answers are possible. One is that it doesn't matter what description is used. The second is that the description reflects the user who determines its application. The important point is that whether it is learning, knowledge management or performance support, it enables people to do their jobs more effectively.

Time and speed to market

The emergence of effective e-learning will lead to a blurring of boundaries. This phenomenon will emerge in a number of forms. Effective e-learning may also assist us in managing (if that is the right word) the constraints of time. Time has certainly emerged as the new scarce resource.

Each year in April the Chartered Institute of Personnel and Development holds a Human Resources Development Conference in London. The conference attracts a large number of delegates, and the associated exhibition even more visitors. Taking advantage of the opportunities of the new technology in 2002, the CIPD held an on-line poll at the exhibition. Visitors to the exhibition stand were asked 'What is the most important training problem facing you in your organisation?' They were offered four alternative answers. 330 people participated, and the results are set out in Table 8.

Obviously this is a far from perfect sample – it reflects the views of those who attended the annual CIPD exhibition and were sufficiently interested to vote. For this reason they can be regarded as a sophisticated and committed cross-section of the profession. Two implications of the result of the poll are of interest. First, the option that attracted the most support was the one that focused on the learner. The second implication is that time is emerging as a scarce resource in training. There is ample evidence to support this view emerging elsewhere in the training scene.

The 2002 CIPD Survey *Who Learns at Work?*[4] was based on 750 telephone interviews of people who had received training. They were also asked if they had turned down training opportunities offered by the employer. If they had done so, the main reason given was that respondents were too busy at work – a result that was reflected in a parallel survey of the opinions of training managers.

A more powerful result emerged from the CIPD 2003 Training and Development Survey.[5] Respondents here were training managers, and they were asked to identify the major barriers to learning. 'Pressure of time' attracted a 91.1 per cent response – well ahead of 'Lack of resources' at 42.0 per cent.

If time is the scarce resource, then speed to market must be an attractive concept. This is a term that has emerged from manufacturing – and particularly the concept of lean manufacturing. Vincent Bozzone, a USA-based specialist in this area who has written a book with the title *Speed to Market*,[6] describes it in the following terms (p.xvii):

> *Whether you call it lean manufacturing, quick-response manufacturing, cycle-time compression, speed to market, or whatever other terms you choose, improving performance and profitability in job shops and custom manufacturing businesses boils down to cutting lead time. This is the single most effective strategy you can follow to strengthen your company's competitive position, increase profits, and secure the future of your business – bar none. Cutting lead time – or more accurately, customer wait time – is the essence of lean manufacturing in make-to-order manufacturing businesses.*

Table 8 / Responses to the question 'What is your organisation's most pressing training problem?'

Time for the learner to receive training	*38 per cent*
Pressure on budgets and costs	*29 per cent*
Designing training programmes that meet the needs of the business	*27 per cent*
Ensuring the quality of training provision	*6 per cent*

Much of the 'speed to market' discussion is about the production processes – continuing improving, scheduling, etc. – that a manufacturing organisation needs to implement to build this form of competitive advantage. However, as is so often the case, an approach developed in another field offers a new perspective for the training professional.

It will be seen that two different concepts are emerging here – though both are concerned with time. The first, and it will reappear powerfully in Chapter 6 where modularisation of training will be considered, is the need to save time: this is the need to deliver training activities in a way that minimises the amount of time that the learner has to spend away from other tasks in the workplace. This has always been presented as one of the most powerful arguments for e-learning. The learner can access material in relevant 'bite-size' chunks at a time of his or her choosing. Speed to market looks at a different issue: when a need for improved skills or knowledge is identified – whether by the organisation or the individual – the intervention needs to be delivered as quickly as possible. In a modern organisation if new skills or knowledge are needed they are likely to be needed now.

Consider the term 'customer wait time' and its implications for the trainer. Here it is easy to see the consequences of a failure to achieve a rapid training response and its implications for the customer.

The following is an extract from a letter which the author received from London Underground. It is not often that an organisation tells a customer that their problems arise because of a failure of training!

> *I am writing further to your letter in which you mention difficulties at our station at Paddington. Firstly let me apologise for any inconvenience you may have suffered.*
>
> *We do strive to keep our Booking Offices open at all advertised times, but there are times when, despite the best efforts of our staff, there is no one available to do so. The most common cause is staff shortage.*
>
> *We are currently striving to train as many Station Assistants as possible to become Booking Office trained, but there are limited spaces on training courses, and some are not able to attain the very high pass mark we set.*

The establishment of processes that allow learners to access information, rapidly, and at the right time, is attractive. This would permit a move to take place from 'just-in-case' learning and training to 'just-in-time'. However, a more powerful concept is personalisation or 'just-for-you' training. This is the third area where e-learning has a still unrealised contribution to make to learning in organisations. It is considered next.

Personalisation/market of one

The idea that learning and training should be built around individuals' needs, their circumstances and their capabilities is nothing new. Good teachers and good instructors do it all the time. Problems can arise if the instructor is inflexible and sticks too rigidly to a prior agenda, as the following example illustrates.

The Annual Conference of the University Forum for Human Resource Development, an international event, was held in Edinburgh in 2002. The main social event was a *ceilidh*, a gathering that featured Scottish country dancing, with music delivered by a band that offered instructions on the dances. One of the delegates was an experienced Scottish dancer based at an Edinburgh University, while several others could vaguely recall dancing classes from their schooldays. The rest – particularly the overseas delegates – were nowhere. The result was chaos on the floor, with couples and formations unable to keep up with the moves, and the occasion disintegrated with laughter. It was marvellous fun but ineffective. What was required of the band was an adjustment in their repertoire. Instead of proceeding through a sequence of ever-more complicated dances they should have played the *Strip the Willow* (a simple and popular dance) three times in succession, followed it with three Virginia reels, and allowed the dancers to build up confidence. They should have seen what was happening and flexed their approach around the learners. They had the capacity to do this in a way that dancing to music played on the radio could not.

As training professionals we can see the humour in this situation, but there is a serious point to be made. Our traditional approach to learning is based on instruction which can be unresponsive and rigid. We know that good trainers, teachers and lecturers do adapt and flex their styles to take account of learners' responses. Good trainers encourage interaction and test learners' understanding throughout. However, such approaches are trainer - rather than learner-centred.

What is new and exciting are the potential opportunities that e-learning offers for what can be described as personalisation or customisation round the individual: the possibility that learners could receive material that reflects their preferred way of absorbing information. The concept is a compelling one and is being explored and implemented in other fields. Some luxury cars how have gearboxes that can adapt automatically over time to the preferred driving habits of the owner. However, personalisation and customisation in e-learning is currently an ambition rather than a reality. A recent study that was undertaken to map the approaches under consideration by suppliers of e-learning has demonstrated limited results to date. An extract from the resulting article is reproduced below.[7]

Customising the learning experience

The underlying proposition is that technology allows for sophisticated ways of customising the delivery of material to match the individual learner's style. In practice, few of the suppliers of e-learning were doing this to a high level, though more planned to develop the capacity of their various systems to accommodate differing learner styles. At the most basic level, customisation of this type allows for the material to be presented in the commissioning company's format, with company logos, and trainees' names inserted at appropriate stages. The next level of customisation is learner tracking, which involves setting a syllabus and guiding learners in a way that reflects their base knowledge and rate of progress, building in adaptive testing and different remedial paths. Some will add in extra content, or suggest links to other materials.

The most advanced systems that were quoted used inference engines: intelligence agents to record learner activity in order to provide future signposts. Some would alter the initial screen (or portal) to reflect a learner's preference for different sorts of information or different layouts. Not all providers offer this type of technological customisation, but others were intending to move in this direction.

A number of suppliers and corporate providers of e-learning saw the first opportunity to customise the e-learning experience at the pre-learning stage. Typically, a course menu would be presented to indicate the learning appropriate to the individual's level or position and/or his or her prior learning experiences. The techniques quoted here involved a variety of pre-assessment, and pre-testing, or the provision of the appropriate learning modules related to the company's competence model, where each learner's current level had been assessed through 360-degree feedback. Others stressed that it was for the learner to choose between alternative modules.

A distinction between 'customisation' and 'personalisation'

During the discussions vendors were specifically asked what was being done for the individual learner. He or she will often get his/her name in the congratulatory messages around achievement, have individual progress logged, and potentially follow different remedial paths as different parts of the material present difficulties. With the technologically advanced systems, his or her preferences for presentational style will be calculated, so for example a visual learner will have more material presented in a visual format.

These methods provide attractive ways of making e-learning more relevant to meeting corporate training needs and also to the individual learner. And they are being actively researched and enhanced by the vendors we contacted. This distinction between customisation (round the needs of the organisational situation) and personalisation (round the needs of the individual learner) is likely to grow in importance. It helps to clarify the concepts and to guide future purchasers of e-learning toward the possibilities that are becoming available to those who would like to invest in more relevant and effective e-learning.

Many of the vendors contacted argued that the above considerations may become redundant; they had moved on to providing blended learning, which can build in all the opportunities for personalising and customising e-learning, and a few more.

Blending, it is suggested, allows for a rich mix of material to be presented in the best way for each part of a programme. Cognitive material, the basic facts and 'must know' can be presented in an electronic format, pre-assessing knowledge to offer only new facts, and testing achievements when 'must know' is important. Links and further levels of detail can be offered to more able learners, to stimulate wider thinking and deepen knowledge. Interaction and debate, to apply the learning to the context in which the learner operates, can be added via e-mail, discussion groups, chatrooms, virtual tutorials and phone lines to experts.

Add to this mix the opportunity to meet in live tutorials, with experts, and to participate in practical exercises to put skills into practice, and it is felt that you end up with the best of all possible learning worlds.

The overall impression from the study dialogue is that some progress is taking place – but that there is a long way to go. Generally, progress in e-learning to date has been driven by the available technology and not by learning considerations. Some hard issues need to be addressed: customisation and personalisation are recognised as laudable aims by vendors and suppliers. There are however questions as to whether the features currently provided by vendors actually increase learning effectiveness. Adopting corporate house styles and logos may be attractive but have little impact on learning. Learner tracking and inference engines are definite system enhancements but are predicated on the assumption that people learn through the absorption of information – this is just one of a number of perspectives on how people learn. Given a fundamental requirement to take account of different leaning needs and situations, the concept of blended learning has great appeal. Much more elaboration, and a constructive dialogue between vendors and trainers, will be required, however, to ensure that the concept is grounded in reality.

Generally, as can be seen from the summary above, progress on personalisation and customi-sation is minimal. There is much more heat than light. An examination of activity re-emphasises a powerful theme behind this book: e-learning is about learning, not technology. Those who care about learning must grasp the agenda.

Is e-learning a different model of learning?

The previous discussion demonstrates the power of e-learning and the contribution that it can make. Clearly, to date e-learning has demonstrated only a fraction of its potential. It can offer a vital, hitherto unavailable, enabling mechanism which can make learner-focus a reality. How this can be done, whether using the new technology or through more traditional methods, will form the third Part of the book, beginning with the next chapter. However, the blurring of bound-aries, new opportunities for speed to market when time is the scarce resource and opportunities for customisation and personalisation could transform the world of the trainer.

Is what is happening so profound that it should totally alter our conception of learning? Time will tell: e-learning certainly creates possibilities which would not have even been dreamed of ten years ago. *How Do People Learn?*[8] asked if e-learning is fundamentally different. Has an entirely new model emerged? It came to the following conclusions (p.52):

The components of e-learning could be defined as:

- multi-way communication amongst learners and between learners and experts
- hypertextual rather than linear presentation of material
- integrated access to resources both inside and outside the learning package
- multimedia forms of interaction and presentation of material.

While these elements may have been available individually before, the combination is new. Furthermore, connectivity over distance and time has had a profound effect not just in terms of learning opportunities, but in a wider social context. Communication through mobile phones has contributed to these changes, but the result is a different expectation about communication and access to information and people.

E-learning then may not require new theories of learning to account for the nature of the learn-ing experience, but may help to create a new paradigm. The paradigm that emerges could be a focus on the learner. The third Part of the book will consider the steps that can be taken to make this a reality in the modern organisation.

REFERENCES AND READING

1   NAUGHTON, J. (2001) *A Brief History of the Future*. London, Phoenix.

2 My acknowledgements to Professor Lynda Gratton of the London Business School for this insight, which she delivered at a CIPD practitioner research seminar held in Bath in 2002. This theme is developed in her book *The Democratic Enterprise: Liberating your business with individual freedom and shared purpose*. London, FT/Prentice Hall, forthcoming 2003.

3 CIPD Training and Development 2002 Survey. London, the CIPD.

4 CIPD (2002) *Who Learns at Work?* CIPD Survey Report. London, the CIPD.

5 CIPD Training and Development 2003 Survey. London, the CIPD.

6 BOZZONE, V. (2001) *Speed to Market: Lean manufacturing for job shops*, 2nd edition. New York, AMACOM; p.xvii.

7 This material previously appeared in an article by Jennifer Taylor and Martyn Sloman entitled 'Customising the learning experience' in *Human Resources Decisions International* 2003 (pp.9–11). We are grateful to the publishers for permission to reproduce their material.

8 REYNOLDS, J., CALEY, L. and MASON, R. (2002) *How Do People Learn?* Research Report produced by Cambridge Programme for Industry for the CIPD.

Part 3

From aspiration to implementation

6

The new agenda for trainers

One member of the new management team was a direct, determined individual who was keen to demonstrate his authority. He decided that it would be a good idea to recruit top MBA students from leading business schools. My investigations suggested that this quality of candidate would only be attracted by a well-designed job with a recognised importance to the business area. An exchange with the businesses showed that they were neither able to identify such jobs nor warm towards MBA entrants in the first place. Thus, finding myself between a rock and a hard place, I decided to go back to the instigator of the idea. I saw him on the escalator entering the building, rode beside him, and gave him the bad news. His reaction was immediate: 'It's going to *** happen,' he said, 'and the reason it's going to happen is that I say it will *** happen. Got the message, sonny?' I was at somewhat of a loss to know how to proceed from there.

Learning lies firmly in the domain of the individual. This proposition is at the heart of the arguments that are advanced throughout this book. The suggestion therefore that a focus on the learner could be implemented by anyone but the learner may appear paradoxical. In fact, there is plenty that can be done to facilitate and encourage learners, and plenty that can be done to create a climate in which they can learn. Learners need information, guidance and the opportunity to practise. Nor is the classroom a thing of the past. In many cases face-to-face instruction may still prove the most efficient way of providing learning opportunities.

The role of the trainer will be enhanced as learning becomes a source of competitive advantage. The name may change (we can expect the word *learning* increasingly to appear in job and department titles), time and money may be directed towards different objectives, but the opportunities for today's skilled human resource development training professional will increase rather than diminish.

Moreover, many organisations and human resource training departments are already taking steps which recognise these new challenges – as the following case studies demonstrate. It is based on the activities that are currently taking place at the Crown Prosecution Service (CPS). In the course of the research undertaken for this book, the CPS offered some particularly interesting illustrations of the challenges facing the modern training function – first, because the CPS is operating in a particularly demanding high-profile environment; second, because it is adopting a considered and multi-faceted approach in meeting these challenges.

Crown Prosecution Service (1)

Background

The Crown Prosecution Service (CPS) is the public sector body established to prosecute criminal and civil cases within magistrates' and crown courts in the United Kingdom. Some 6,500 staff are employed across 42 geographical areas, which are aligned with the boundaries of the police authorities and headquarters. 2,500 of these staff are lawyers and the CPS could be characterised as the 'largest law firm in the country' – certainly it is the biggest recruiter of lawyers, taking in some 300 lawyers at a range of experience-levels in any one year.

A training department of 25 staff has been established to ensure that the CPS lawyers, associated caseworkers and administrative staff attain and retain the requisite knowledge and skills. Just over half of these staff are based in regional offices and offer a full service to the local areas. Others are responsible for specialist training areas. These include: the co-ordination of lawyer training, including Law Society liaison (a post held by a trained lawyer); management and leadership development; meeting the needs of human resources professionals; and special projects.

There is a continuing need for legal updating for both the lawyers and the caseworkers. The latter are responsible for the preparation of documentation to support the work of the lawyers, a process that requires extensive liaison with the courts and the police authorities. It is possible for some of these staff to receive training to become a 'designated caseworker', which permits them to perform a limited range of functions in the court room.

The CPS is able to call mainly on in-house lawyers to deliver the specialist legal training, both for their fellow lawyers and the caseworkers. Their willingness to perform this training function is a reflection on the generally positive view of training held within the CPS. Many in-house lawyers see training delivery as a development opportunity.

Training needs

The CPS training strategy is agreed each year through the production of an annual training plan, which specifies priorities, targets and resources. Major current priorities include: leadership and management development; IT training on a new case tracking system; management advice and work on early advice and charging. As well as legal training there is a continuing requirement for leadership and management development. The most senior staff, the 42 individuals designated Chief Crown Prosecutors in their areas, recently attended a bespoke programme at Ashridge Management College. Another customised course, aimed at the next level down, was introduced in April 2003: this is based around the skills needs addressed in the course of a 360-degree feedback exercise and has been developed in partnership with a range of suppliers. There are ongoing requirements for training on interpersonal skills (presentation skills, performance feedback, interviewing, etc); most of this training is delivered by the regional training staff.

In addition, training in IT office systems is a continuing requirement, both in respect of standard packages and when systems are updated. A new case tracking system is shortly about to be introduced. One problem is that the sophistication of IT use among staff is variable; although CPS was not one of the early adopters of information technology, now all staff have access to a corporate intranet and all have PCs. This is relatively advanced in the context of the criminal justice.

Training issues
The training objectives that the CPS is seeking to achieve do not differ significantly from those of other organisations of a similar size in both the public and private sectors. There is a need for a more inclusive management style: according to one member of the training function, 'The adversarial style that is prized in the courtroom may not be as effective for internal communication.' There is a continuing need for technical (in this case legal training), and skills and systems updating.

There is, however, a particular level of challenge for the CPS which reflects the nature of its activities. The CPS is a high-profile organisation and its alleged or real mistakes are ruthlessly exposed. Secondly, there is a need to achieve speed to market in training where new government initiatives are introduced. Such initiatives can reflect changing political priorities. Legislation can be under consideration or in preparation for a considerable time and then be brought forward rapidly.

As a result a considerable effort has been invested in two new programmes.

'Speaking-up for Justice', which is CPS's first significant e-learning initiative, reflects the need to disseminate new legislation to a multiplicity of users in a tight timescale. 'Direct Communications with Victims' illustrates the challenges in creating an effective high-level soft-skills intervention where changing circumstances require a different set of behaviours. These are described more fully in the case study continuations below.

Other specialist modules in hand or under consideration concern international crime, the proceeds of crime, and racially aggravated crime. Beyond these examples of demanding delivery problems, CPS's Head of Training and Development, Shelagh Preston, and her colleagues have identified the following challenges facing the training function.

First, there is a desire to shift to a culture where a requirement for skills or knowledge updating does not automatically suggest the creation of a new training course. In part this will be achieved by improved training needs analysis at the time of preparation of the annual plans. In this way attempts are made to ensure that classroom elements are more effectively targeted. Generally, there is an intention to increase the responsibility that the learner takes for his or her own updating.

Second, there are always competing demands on training resources – both cash to pay for the provision of training, and time to deliver the agreed programmes. New initiatives following from legislation can emerge at the same time as a requirement for training to support new office

CASE STUDY continued

systems – and these in turn must compete for attention with ongoing skills updating. Set against this, however, training is seen as important by the CPS, and the challenge facing the training function is one of prioritising and delivery. Effective training is accepted as essential by the organisation.

My thanks to Shelagh Preston and Sharron Hughes for their assistance with the preparation of this case study.

A number of considerations which the CPS is taking into account in determining its approach have already been discussed in the course of the book. These include:

- the need to provide specific technical training
- appropriate use of the Internet (for knowledge, not skills) and a sensible interpretation of blended learning
- competing demands on learner time, which is now the scarce resource
- the need for speed to market, getting training in place against tight timescales
- the need to establish a base of IT skills.

In developing appropriate policies to address these issues, the CPS is moving towards a learner-focus.

What is needed therefore is not a complete rejection of what is happening at present – there is much good practice about. For many organisations the requirement is to proceed with more urgency along the existing direction, and to be more explicit in accepting a learner-focus model. We need to go beyond a desire that the learner must take responsibility for his or her own learning into identifying a wide-ranging set of interventions based on the paradigm of learner-focus. How this can be done will form the subject of the latter part of this chapter.

CASE STUDY CONTINUATION

CPS (2): Speaking up for Justice

The requirement

One of the 1997 manifesto commitments of the incoming Government concerned the need to offer greater protection to 'victims in rape and serious sexual offence trials and for those subject to intimidation including witnesses'. A year later the Home Office published *Speaking up for Justice*, a report on the treatment of vulnerable and intimidated immediate witnesses, including children, in the criminal justice system. The report made 78 recommendations designed to improve the treatment of witnesses. These covered all stages in the process including investigation, pre-trial, trial and post-trial activities. One of the specific recommendations was the requirement for a training needs analysis for those working within the criminal justice system. This was undertaken by the Home Office Justice and Victim's Unit.

This training needs analysis identified three core competencies that were required to implement the recommendations of *Speaking up for Justice*. These were: an ability to identify vulnerable and

CASE STUDY continued

intimidated witnesses; a need to challenge and change current perceptions and attitudes in relation to vulnerable and intimidated witnesses; the capability of delivering a high-quality service to vulnerable and intimidated witnesses. Because the need was important, the timescale for implementation was tight. The module was targeted at 1,300 lawyers.

The approach

The CPS Training Department adopted a blended solution involving both classroom and web-based elements. IQdos, a company that specialises in the production of bespoke e-learning solutions, was contracted to design and deliver the e-learning component. This was intended to allow lawyers to equip themselves with the appropriate knowledge on the treatment of vulnerable and intimidated witnesses: it allows them to access, research and update the information elements at any time. The use of the e-learning module has two other advantages. First, it can be kept up to date as the information component changes (new legislation and developing case law). Second, it offers access to links which contain useful additional information.

The *Speaking up for Justice* e-learning module can be used as a standalone training and information tool. In this way it reflects the blurring between performance management/performance support and learning that was discussed in the previous chapter. The CPS has taken a decision to allow access to its partners who are involved in ensuring the new approach to the treatment of witnesses. These include barristers, court service officials and the police. Those who would benefit from access could have different and less sophisticated technology at their desks (and indeed may be accessing from a designated centre at work or from home). With this multiplicity of users in mind, the module was designed so that high bandwidth is not required. It is hosted in the IQdos server, so the access issues are managed by them.

Within the CPS, as has been noted, the e-learning module forms part of a blended solution. The CPS lawyers and caseworkers participate in a three-day classroom training event. This reinforces the knowledge gained through exercises and case study applications. It concentrates on the skills element and the behavioural/attitudinal elements needed to ensure that greater support is given to vulnerable witnesses.

The responsibility for making this transition (and identifying a wide-ranging set of interventions based on the paradigm of learner-focus) extends far beyond the training department. The role of all human resource development professionals should be to create the conditions under which 'committed individuals who understand the organisation's objectives, have the opportunity to acquire and maintain the requisite skills' (to rephrase part of the definition introduced in Chapter 1, p.14).

CPS (3): Direct communication with victims

The CPS lawyers and caseworkers often have to work on sensitive cases, and their communications with victims and their families can be very demanding and sometimes harrowing. Considerable personal communications skills, empathy and awareness can be required. One example, which is particularly difficult, is when the CPS must tell victims or their families that it is not proceeding with the prosecution, altering or reducing charges, because there is insufficient evidence to proceed with the original charge.

Appropriate treatment of victims and their families can become a high-profile issue particularly in racially aggravated crime. More generally, the treatment of victims is an issue which is receiving international attention. The UN have produced recommendations on the rights of victims.

Better treatment of victims and witnesses emerged as a significant political issue in the UK in the late 1990s, and CPS Training reviewed and redesigned its training in this area.

The approach
The solution adopted by the CPS was to develop, in consultation with a consultancy, ITS Training, a three-day face-to-face training module. The learning objectives for the module are defined as follows. By the end of the events the participants will:

- have an understanding of the legal requirements and restrictions involved in explaining prosecution decisions to victims and families of victims
- have an understanding of their obligations under the scheme and Victim's Charter for explaining prosecution decisions to victims and bereaved families of victims killed as a result of crime
- have identified, practised and received feedback on the core skills for effective face-to-face and written communication with victims and families of victims.

In some respects these may appear to be typical skills training objectives: a heavy concentration on communication and feedback skills in an appropriate context. Two elements make this a particularly complex event, however. The first concerns the potential delicacy of the relationship with the victim or family. The timing of the arrival of written communication – the distress caused if a letter arrives on the anniversary of a death – is one illustration. Under certain circumstances the personal safety of the person giving unwelcome news can be an issue (eg meetings with victims).

The second key element is that new approaches and attitudes are required as the communication with victims progressively becomes more open. According to Mark Lake, the CPS Project Manager responsible for developing the programme, 'The aim now is to give as much information as you can – to some this is seen as a reversal of previous policies.'

Against this background the three-day module is built around information sessions, case studies, role play and feedback. Diversity issues are considered; appropriate forms and timing of address

CASE STUDY continued

are reviewed, attitudes are considered, and stereotyping challenged – for example, distinguishing between 'deserving' and 'undeserving' victims. Confidence is built through role playing. In Mark Lake's words, 'It's as stressful playing the victim as playing the lawyer.'

My thanks to Mark Lake for his assistance with the preparation of this case study. For a fuller discussion of this programme, see the article that appeared in *Personnel Management* in August 2002.[1]

Traditionally, 'training' interventions have been seen as the direct responsibility or accountability of a training manager. They include events based in the training room, e-learning opportunities, on-the-job training, project-based or action learning and learning from coaching or mentoring. One sensible interpretation of the fashionable term 'blended learning' is the co-ordination of these interventions to achieve an integrated and balanced whole. However, these 'training' interventions form only a part of the activities needed to create the appropriate conditions for the willing learner to flourish. The whole range of broader human resource activities will influence the climate for learning. Indeed, it would be hard to point to a human resource intervention, from whatever source, which does not have some effect on skills acquisition and retention – however indirect. Responsibility for the climate for learning extends far beyond those who carry the word training in their job title.

However, given the main focus and the readership for this book, this and the following two chapters will concentrate mainly on the activities that should be undertaken by the human resource development/learning and training professional. For convenience this role will be described as that of a 'trainer' as, despite the shift in focus to learning, 'trainer' remains the term most commonly in use at the time of writing. This chapter will next consider what is happening to the core elements of the role.

The role of the trainer

There is an almost universal recognition that the role of trainer is changing. A number of recent reports have addressed aspects of this transition. Two of these are summarised in the inset sections below.

Summary

The role of the trainer

In 2002 the CIPD invited Nottingham Business School to investigate the impact on the training function of the shift to the knowledge economy. This was defined as one where the focus was on 'the importance of know-how, innovation, design and branding and the social processes that create these, to the generation of a firm's competitive advantage'.[2]

The report identified a range of significant issues including the following:

- Responsibility for learning and development is increasingly being placed on managers and employees rather than training professionals. This has implications for the role of the training contribution, with more importance being attached to acting as learning facilitator and strategic partner rather than training provider.

- It is unsafe to assume either that managers and other employees possess the necessary competence or that they will adopt positive attitudes towards their new responsibilities.

- The immediate and medium-term contribution of training and training professionals therefore needs to focus on developing the competence and motivation of managers and other employees in relation to managing learning and development. Training professionals must play a crucial role in changing the organisational culture to one where line managers understand and act on their responsibility to support the learning and development of the employees whom they manage.

- Informal and work-based learning is of increasing importance in the knowledge economy. Highly developed learning skills are necessary to maximise the potential offered by conscious and deliberate learning through work.

- Developing these skills in the workforce requires training practitioners to concentrate their attention on learning processes, rather than the content of learning, much more than in the past. Effective learning process design will make a significant contribution to developing the skills of learning.

- This supports an idea that many training professionals have been advocating – that is, of the trainer as facilitator rather than instructor. This may be particularly true when dealing with knowledge workers who are, themselves, subject specialists and who are highly demanding of training.

Summary

The role of the function

Aligning training with business strategy was explored in a report by the Institute for Employment Studies (IES) and published as *Resourcing the Training and Development Function*.[3] In their research they found (p.xii) that 'the shifting organisational forms of training, coupled with multiple delivery methods, are not leading to a single new role for the trainer, but rather an array of different role demands'.

The roles that were predicted to increase involved the trainer as a facilitator, an organisational change agent, or a policy strategist. Other important but more specialist roles included evaluation, business planning, training design, outsourced services management, external benchmarking, training needs identification and carrier development support. The direct delivery of formal training was the only role thought to become less important.

Generally, there is an emerging consensus on the role of the training function: it will become more demanding and more varied; there will be increasing divergence and specialism. Some trainers will work as strategic-facilitators, carrying responsibility for aligning activities with business objectives. Others could become e-learning designers or remain classroom deliverers of interpersonal skills training.

The new business drivers, reinforced by technology will demand rapid changes and responses in the skills sets needed by trainers. Using the systematic training model (identify, design, deliver and evaluate: see Chapter 3, pp.23–25) as a basis to build lists of competencies will not capture the subtleties of the opportunities opening up and the skills required. Indeed, it may be used to absolve indifferent management from discharging its responsibilities.

An alternative starting point is to return to the analysis presented in Chapter 3. This suggested that people learn for work, at work and through work. A fair assumption would be that 'for work' mainly takes place in the education system. The 'at work' skills would see the trainer as enricher, questioner and creator of learning communities. The 'through work' skills would see the trainer as a mediator of time and resources and a supporter of teams.[4]

Others will have different views on what skills should go in the 'at work' and 'through work' boxes. The possibilities for debate are considerable. What is important is that they start from a focus on the learner rather than the perspective of the trainer.

However the role is construed, whoever does it, and whatever it is called, certain basic activities will need to take place. Many of these involve initiatives and tasks that all trainers will recognise. They will be considered in the next two chapters. However, if the paradigm of learner-focus is to move from aspiration to reality, a different type of intervention (learner-centred interventions) will be needed.

This brings us firmly into the practical territory of what can be done and what needs to be done. Before embarking on this process, it is however helpful to summarise the arguments that have been presented in this book so far. These are set out in diagrammatic form as Figure 6. It can be seen that

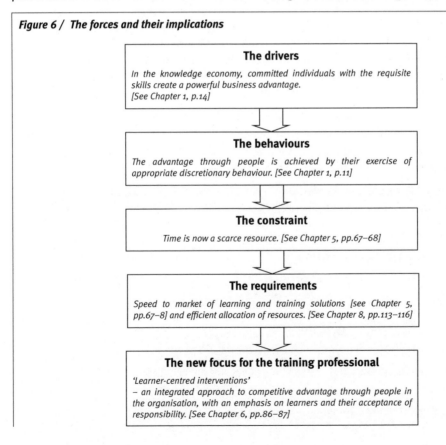

Figure 6 / The forces and their implications

The drivers

In the knowledge economy, committed individuals with the requisite skills create a powerful business advantage.
[See Chapter 1, p.14]

The behaviours

The advantage through people is achieved by their exercise of appropriate discretionary behaviour. [See Chapter 1, p.11]

The constraint

Time is now a scarce resource. [See Chapter 5, pp.67–68]

The requirements

Speed to market of learning and training solutions [see Chapter 5, pp.67–8] and efficient allocation of resources. [See Chapter 8, pp.113–116]

The new focus for the training professional

'Learner-centred interventions'
– an integrated approach to competitive advantage through people in the organisation, with an emphasis on learners and their acceptance of responsibility. [See Chapter 6, pp.86–87]

there is a logical chain from the new perspectives (competition through people exercising discretionary behaviour) through to the learner-centred interventions which will be considered next.

Learner-centred interventions

This book is about the new paradigm and a focus on the learner. To repeat the description presented in the Introduction:

> *Interventions and activities which are intended to improve knowledge and skills in organisations will increasingly focus on the learner. Emphasis will shift to the individual learner (or the team), and he or she will be encouraged to take more responsibility for his or her learning. Efforts will be made to develop a climate which supports effective and appropriate learning. Such interventions and activities will form part of an integrated approach to creating competitive advantage through people in the organisation.*

Few training professionals would resist the suggestion that their role in the organisation should be reviewed. Best modern training practice is always evolving and changing. The Investors in People framework (see Chapter 1, reference 1) could fairly be said to express the essence of an approach which reflects the systematic training model. There is nothing wrong with this: it has its place. What is argued here is that we need to go beyond such constructs, adopt a new paradigm, and develop an approach which focuses on the learner. In short, is it possible to identify and implement learner-centred interventions or activities?

What is described in most of the remainder of this chapter is the result of a short feasibility project undertaken at the CIPD during the Spring of 2003. Twelve organisations co-operated in this project. They are listed at the end of this chapter together with a reference to the research report.[5] Gratitude is due to these organisations and their training managers for their openness and their willingness to share ideas and information.

The starting point for the project was a recognition that if there is to be a planned shift to a focus on the learner, some tangible activities must be taking place. One of the criticisms of the 'learning organisation' advanced in Chapter 2 is that it was a fine concept which was never grounded in reality. What can organisations do, and what are they doing?

Participating organisations were presented with a list of interventions and activities which could potentially shift towards a focus on the learner. These are shown in the text box below.

LEARNER-CENTRED INTERVENTIONS

- efforts to ensure that individuals are clear about the skills that are required in their jobs
- personal responsibility for managing learning is an explicit part of the job
- recognition of the committed learner takes place
- some sort of assessment of skills/capabilities on arrival
- some sort of 'learning contract' between the individual and the employer, as part of the recruitment/induction process
- much more just-for you and just-in-time training

- training interventions delivered in a more modular form so that less time may be spent in any session
- line managers trained to act as support/coaches
- provision of appropriate time to learn
- formal recognition and acknowledgement of the role of the supportive line manager
- new approaches to measurement and reporting on learning outcomes
- changing role and title of training managers
- new budgetary arrangements
- increasing emphasis on competency frameworks
- senior manager involvement in learning/training going beyond declarations of support.

Organisations were asked three questions about these activities:

- How significant is this factor in terms of its potential contribution to the effectiveness of the learning/training efforts in your organisation?
- Are these activities a subject of current review/discussion in your organisation?
- To what extent do these activities take place in your organisation at present?

All the organisations in the study recognised the relevance of the shift to learning from training; all thought that this was a desirable objective. All wanted to achieve something beyond well-managed and effective training delivered by the training department. All the training managers were clear on their intentions and the reasons that led them to act as they did. For example, one of the best expressions of the shift to learning and training and its link with discretionary behaviour was offered by two human resource managers from Hilton Hotels Ireland.

'Because of the nature of the business we can't train everyone to do everything. The emphasis is on getting people to learn within the environment where they work, and getting them to adapt and apply that knowledge.'

'In the hospitality industry, probably more than any other service industry, every customer [guest] has different expectations. There is no way we can train for every eventuality. We want our staff to be spontaneous and react and respond to guest expectations.'

Lorna McKee, Area HR Manager, Hilton Belfast

'Training and learning is like hearing and listening. You can hear but not listen; you have to take an active decision to listen and that's down to the individual.'

'Now we say that, through appraisals and their own training needs analysis, the business must tell us what training is needed. We discuss with them how to deliver it. This emphasis is not just a good thing: it is essential. If someone just turns up for training they will have no commitment.'

Clare Macleod, HR Manager, Hilton Dublin

Ambitions and focus varied. Inevitably there were differences which reflected the size of the organisations and the type of business: both determine the nature of competition through people and the positioning of the development effort.

However, there were some consistent themes that emerged from the study regardless of size and sector. The first concerned the need to create an effective platform if a move from training to learning was to take place. Two issues emerged here: one was support from the board and senior management; a second was the need to meet what might be described as the essential obligations of the training department.

The need for senior management support will come as no surprise – how often have we heard that? The survey indicated that this factor could be best described as a necessary precondition before any of the others could be delivered. Generally what the study organisations had to report was good news: there was wide recognition of the importance of developing people and its links to business performance. However, there is a subtler point at issue here: when the emphasis shifts from learning to training, the board may be supportive, but are they necessarily sure of the implications of what they have endorsed? The importance of this point becomes apparent when the impact of these changes on the role of the training professional, as seen by others in the organisation, is considered.

The second issue, the need for the training department to meet its essential obligations, is straightforward. In almost every organisation there are some basic training requirements: these could include induction training, basic IT training and in some cases training to meet regulatory or statutory requirements. The training function will not be able to move on to its wider strategic ambitions unless these obligations have been met effectively and are seen to have been met. Only then will deployable resources of budget and trainer's time become available. In this sense the function needs to earn the right to move forward.

Once this basic platform is in place, it is possible to advance. It is possible to move from a position where individuals expect training to be delivered to them to one where individuals will take responsibility for their own knowledge and skills development. What are the steps that the organisations are taking? Where are they putting their efforts? Here it is helpful to return to the list set out in the text box above. All the organisations in the study recognised these factors as legitimate and relevant. In practice, however, the factors can be subdivided into a number of categories.

Although the emphasis varied across different organisations, three activities seemed to be high on everyone's list. These were: first, line managers' increasing expectations to act as coaches and to receive training to ensure that they had the requisite coaching skills; second, a growing emphasis on competency frameworks; third, efforts to deliver training efforts in a more modular form. These three together could be said to be the focus of current attention and action.

Coaching

The role and importance of coaching is considered in Chapter 7. Coaching has been a recognised feature of individual development in organisations for some time. As a result, coaching skills have been a feature of the course menu offered by most training departments.

What is new is the growing recognition that coaching is a near-essential component in the armoury of the manager skills.'

The greater emphasis on coaching activities of line managers manifests itself in several respects. First, there is a more extensive provision of training; second, such training is not exclusively the preserve of the volunteer learner – to different degrees the acquisition of coaching skills is less likely to be seen as an optional activity; third, initiatives may be in place to ensure that line managers do undertake the necessary coaching. Some illustrations from the study are set out as quotations below.

> *'Every two weeks all associates are expected to participate in a discussion with their managers known as a 10/10. This is a 20-minute conversation with ten minutes' input from the manager and ten minutes' input from the associate. It is expected that development discussions reflect the competencies and that feedback is supported by behavioural examples.'*

> *'The general support and coaching skills for managers are therefore of recognised importance to the development of the business.'*

> *'Coaching is but one manifestation of the skills set required. This capability must be delivered in a way that is appropriate to the situation: non-directive for the high performer and in a more directive approach for the low performer. Coaching skills will be a major focus of the development curriculum for managers that is being developed. This initiative has support at all levels, including the highest.'*

> Kevin Hogarth, Director of International Resourcing, Capital One Bank (Europe)

> *'One of the biggest successes, which secured a National Training Award, concerns the Sales Through Service Lead Generation programme. This was driven by the changing business requirements concerning the sale of insurance products. Classroom training was a success, but results tailed off after time when participants were back in the job. Accordingly, two coaches were identified and attached to the training department to support branches in their efforts.'*

> *'This proved so successful that seven "branch coaches" were appointed after internal recruitment. They concentrate mainly on sales but work as performance coaches assisting staff to meet all aspects of their jobs. For an organisation of this size this is a big resource commitment.'*

> Helen Cairns, Business Manager, HR Training and Development, Dunfermline Building Society

Competency frameworks

Again, competencies have been a feature of progressive human resource development for more than a decade. Competencies can be defined as the behaviour that employees must have or must acquire to input into a situation in order to achieve high levels of performance.[6] The competency frameworks that organisations in the study are introducing have a clear purpose. They are designed to indicate what the good performer should be doing. A key part of the way in which they will be judged is their use as a means for an individual to identify his or her developmental needs. This process will take place in conjunction with the line manager, but the framework should be sufficiently transparent as to be understood by the employee alone. The potential contribution of electronic technology (linked to e-learning) is evident.

In this sense competency systems are a signal to individuals of what is required of them. They act as a link between the business model and individual contribution; they signpost appropriate discretionary behaviour. They then can be used to identify learning gaps.

Given this link with the business model, it is not surprising that almost all the study organisations developed their competency frameworks themselves. They need to own them rather than have them imposed from outside. Some illustrations from study organisations are set out as quotations below.

'The management committee of the corporate and commercial business discussed the leadership behaviours required to drive the business forward. In the course of this investigation they identified five behaviours and recognised that they should be extended beyond leadership to cover a whole range of management activities. The five behaviours were: fast-moving, results-driven, innovative, customer-centred, engaging. They are known by the semi-acronym "Fried Rice".'

'The behaviours are integral to Zurich performance management/review system. Traditionally this review, leading into a salary assessment, has been based on business outcomes. However, all staff now have 20 per cent of the performance assessed against the five behaviours. Moreover, those staff who are managing other people or who can be identified as those who carry out another's appraisals have an additional 10 per cent of their performance assessed in terms of how well they discharge these management responsibilities. Three component activities have been identified: performance management, talent management, learning and development.'

Ian Canning, Head of Learning and Development, Corporate and Government,
Zurich Financial Services

'We have a well-established competency framework which was originally developed in the USA involving the support of external consultants. The framework is used for the selection process and in performance/development reviews. The performance review is based on 50 per cent outcomes and 50 per cent competencies and a formal development discussion must take place at least twice a year.'

Kevin Hogarth, Director of International Resourcing, Capital One Bank (Europe)

Modular training activities

Many organisations in the sample reported that they were delivering basic training in shorter modules so that staff did not need to be away from the workplace for long periods. Typically, two-day courses were seen as the maximum. Some respondents were delivering soft-skills modules in two- or even one-hour blocks.

Is this tendency connected with the move from training to learning? Or is it simply good training practice in an environment when time is the new scarce resource? There is an argument that it is a necessary component of the shift to learning if it offers the learner and manager more choice, takes away the pressures, and makes it easier to learn. However, as the illustrative quotations below demonstrate, modularisation can be demanding and difficult to practise, and not always appropriate.

'The training team is attempting to deliver management and interpersonal management skills in chunks of one hour – for example, supervisory skills, personal assistant skills and others have all been modularised in this form.'

'This poses a considerable challenge for the training function. There is a need to get a certain amount of information across in a given time – professional standards may be pushed to the limits. Sequencing of material can be very difficult, if not impossible. (Some participants may arrive for module 4 having missed module 3.) Much of this modularised training is delivered first thing in the morning, at lunchtime or immediately after work.'

Sue Lenkowksi, Training and Development Manager, Irwin Mitchell

'In some respects it is easier to arrange cover for one day than one hour. In hospital a loss of a person for an hour can be very evident in an emergency.'

Simon Tisdale, Head of Training and Development, Salford Royal Hospitals NHS Trust

If these three (coaching, competency frameworks and modularisation) were the activities that absorbed most of the current attention, other factors were as important in achieving a cultural shift towards the self-reliant learning. These included the following.

First, efforts to ensure that individuals are clear about the skills that are required in their jobs. It was hoped that such clarity would emerge from a well-designed and well-communicated competency framework reinforced through an effective performance management system. Other related initiatives, which for most organisations were at the aspiration stage, were: personal responsibility for managing learning as an explicit part of the job; recognition for the committed learner; the introduction of learning contracts as part of the recruitment/induction process; formal recognition and acknowledgement of the supportive line manager; some sort of skills or capability assessment on arrival – which was also seen as a consequence of an embedded competency framework.

Finally, some factors were recognised as important but were not receiving any significant attention. One was the provision of more 'just for you'/'just in time' training. Many of the training managers in the study recognised the need to meet organisational requirements with greater speed to market, and all recognised the need to avoid the blanket provision of training with resultant waste. None however felt that they had the information base nor the capability to customise or personalise training for the individual as opposed to the work-group. At this stage this could only be achieved through the expensive option of individual coaching.

Two of the listed factors were recognised as of relevance for the long term but were receiving no attention. These concerned the allocation and measurement of resources. They were: new approaches to measurement of and reporting on learning outcomes and new budgetary arrangements. If, as will be argued in Chapter 8, new approaches will be required to monitor learning as opposed to training, the conceptual thinking, let alone practical implementation, is yet to begin.

It is important to recognise, in reviewing interventions and actions, that only so much can be done. Each intervention requires planning to determine how it can be delivered appropriately, and energy and time and resources to make it happen.

Good judgement is required on what is possible and what is appropriate at any given time. In moving to place more responsibility on individuals and on managers, to some extent a training department is risking its own credibility. This is where senior management support is critical. As one training manager in the survey, Sue Lenkowski of the solictors Irwin Mitchell, put it,

One of the barriers to making that shift is the outside perception of the role of the training function. If we try to transfer ownership for training, people will say 'But that's your job!' They will put the onus back to me arguing that they haven't the time.

It is possible to redefine the capabilities of the effective training managers in terms of what is required to manage this transition. They need a clear vision of what they wish to achieve, to have secured the support of business leadership for this vision, to understand the culture of their organisation, to know what initiatives will be effective, and to secure the resources to deliver the initiatives efficiently and effectively.

Is the above simply good training management as it would have been recognised a decade ago? To an extent the answer must be yes. As has been noted, some activities and initiatives can be regarded as no more than well-designed delivery. However, the results from the study suggest that more is at stake. There is indeed a move in best-practice organisations from training to learning. The role and sometimes the title is changing.

Although this does not come from an organisation which participated in the study, the following expresses well what is at issue. A director from the Ministry of Defence was describing a reason for changing his team's name from Defence Management Training to Defence Business Learning.[7]

As we looked at the challenges ahead for a government department wishing to engage in continuous improvement and increased professionalism in support of the Armed Services, we found the 'training' label becoming unhelpful. We were still finding people claiming they were being 'sent for training', as they might be sent for a punishing five-mile run. Whereas we wanted to engage with people and help them find the best way that they could learn more quickly what they needed to do their jobs better, immediately and in the future. We wanted our customers to be clear that they were taking significant responsibility themselves for our joint endeavours. We wanted our staff to focus clearly on the outcomes of our work – the application of learning back at the workplace. We wanted to create a partnership where our sponsors, staff and customers identify from a range of options what is the most rewarding blend for them – from text, on-site session, seminar-based events, or e-learning. My management team thought this was best signalled to everyone by the change of name and our new strapline 'learning, to make a difference'.

In summary, many modern training departments are engaged in an intensive effort to change the approach used to identify, support and manage learning. However, this move from training to learning is demanding and painstaking. It will be achieved gradually. One is reminded of the verse from the Prophet Isaiah:

For precept must be upon precept, precept upon precept;

line upon line, line upon line;

here a little, and there a little.

(Isaiah 28:10)

Disturbingly, in many Bible commentaries this verse carries the warning 'Hebrew uncertain, meaning obscure'!

E-learning and learner-centred interventions

Having completed this brief review of current progress on learner-centred interventions, it is helpful to return to one of the central questions of this book. What can e-learning contribute to learning and training in the modern organisation?

Quite simply, e-learning – the new opportunity that has arisen from the connectivity of computers – is an enabling tool of enormous as yet untapped potential.

Consider the three activities which were identified above as being at the heart of the current agenda of the training managers interviewed in the course of the study: the introduction or extension of competency frameworks, the modularisation of training provision and the development of coaching capacity. How can e-learning help in these cases?

On competency frameworks it can be seen immediately that the instant access and transmission of up-to-date information is of considerable benefit. In this instance what we call e-learning may be little more than an extended filing cabinet. It is however possible to offer web-based modules (the 'stuff', p.51) linked with many of these competencies. These can be used for self-assessment and to signpost the learner to many external sources of internal and external information and assistance. Tracking of progress can also assist – and this is important – all except the most self-confident learner will require support or assistance in moving from such systems to embark on effective personal development. It is even easier to see how e-learning can assist modularisation. Indeed, this has been one of the most powerful arguments advanced for its introduction. 'Bite-size chunks' has entered the training lexicon to describe the short modules that can be made available on an individual's personal computer.

However, how can e-learning assist in the development of a coaching provision? Here any connection is less evident if it exists at all. True, it is possible to communicate electronically across the organisation what may be required or desired. The information content of a coaching course may be stripped out and made available in advance; in this way classroom time can be reduced and used for the face-to-face element. But that is the extent of its contribution. Mercifully, this now seems to be accepted and, as has been noted, the rise of the term 'blended learning' seems a recognition of the limitations of technology.

Using technology for learning and training is however not simply about delivery of material. As the illustration of the provision of competencies shows, many of the new opportunities that arise are concerned with a changing interface between the user and the organisation. E-learning will never be more than a component part of the job of the training professional. But it has always been recognised that this component part extends beyond delivery. In the final two chapters some other features of the role of the training function will be considered: these concern the delivery of value to the organisation and demonstrating the results.

REFERENCES AND READING

1   HAMMOND, D. (2002) 'A close hearing', *People Management*, Vol 8, No. 17, August; p.24.
2   STEWART, J. and TANSLEY, C. (2002) *Training in the Knowledge Economy*. CIPD Research Report; p.ix. See also SCHRAMM, J. (2002) 'A hard lesson to learn', *People Management*, Vol 8, No. 8, April; pp.32–34.

3 CARTER, A., HIRSH, W. and ASTON, J. (2003) *Resourcing the Training and Development Function.* IES Report 390.

4 I am indebted to Karen Jaques for this insight.

5 Aearo, Capital One Bank (Europe plc), Crown Prosecution Service, DARA, Dunfermline Building Society, Hilton Hotels Ireland, INA Bearings, Irwin Mitchell, London Borough of Hammersmith and Fulham, Marks & Spencer, Salford Royal Hospitals NHS Trust, Zurich Financial Services. See CIPD (2003) 'Focus the learner', Change Agenda.

6 This definition is taken from 'Competency and competency frameworks' – one of a series of *Quick Facts* available from the CIPD at www.cipd.co.uk. This Quick Fact was originally produced by Clare Hogg of Helios Associates Ltd.

7 I am grateful to David Laughrin, Director, Defence Business Learning, for this contribution.

7

Delivering value

One important lever for change was the performance management system. A completed performance appraisal form was essential if the employee was to receive the (often very considerable) annual pay increase. Completion of the paperwork was virtually 100 per cent – but quality was patchy. The development aspect of the review was always neglected and often ignored. The performance objectives set did not confirm to the specific, measurable, attainable, realistic, timebound model, and generally only two or three objectives were set. Much effort was put into training round this SMART model and it was a delight to see the most senior staff in attendance. It was therefore somewhat of a disappointment on reading the completed forms to see that one of them had given a direct subordinate one and only one objective. It read 'Help cover my backside'.

Views on what constitutes the most effective learner-centred interventions, and how they can be delivered, will develop over time. Emerging technology will create new opportunities and new challenges across the whole range of learning and training activities. In these final two chapters, a number of other features of the modern trainer's role will be considered. They will be revisited in the new context of a focus on the learner. For convenience this chapter will concentrate on some aspects of delivering value in the organisation; and the following chapter will consider some of the issues involved in demonstrating value and on the overall place of learning.

In this chapter three topics will be reviewed in turn. First, the place of the instruction and the role of the instructor will be reviewed. Second, some questions surrounding the encouragement and support of learning will be discussed. Third, some practical issues involved in the implementation of e-learning will be presented.

Instruction and beyond

In the early days of e-learning it was all too easy to over-estimate its potential contribution to the future of learning. It sometimes seemed that e-learning was about to do everything bar make the coffee for the break. Consider the following 'futures' scenario – admittedly taken from an educational rather than a corporate setting.

After assembly, the first period is GNVQ Science, in which digital learning materials on the school's intranet features prominently. Currently, pupils are working through these in a three-week block. Uzman works independently on the unit on physical forces and regularly discusses his experiences with other pupils doing this through a virtual community of which he is a member. However, he knows that he can e-mail his science teacher to seek help with any assessment he has not understood. He also knows that, for this lesson, the teacher has prioritised direct support for another group of pupils who are having rather more difficulty with some of the ideas than he is ...

This is an extract from a Department for Education and Skills publication.[1] The report was highly commended by Estelle Morris, the then Education and Skills Minister. It sets out a powerful vision. Equally, it raises some important questions.

Uzman seems a long way from the teenage boys who attended a North London school with my two sons. Left to themselves with a PC and asked to work independently on the unit on physical forces they would have done no such thing. They would have discussed the Arsenal score from the night before (and may well have accessed the site on the web). Getting them back into line would have demanded time from the teacher at the expense of the direct support for the other group of pupils. In short, Uzman is a swot. With this approach he will go far, but the school day needs to be designed round the full range of normal pupils. The role of the teacher may change – and enormous efficiencies may be captured – but good teachers and good teaching will still be required. Exactly the same arguments can be applied to the corporate setting. Whether the specialist is called a trainer or a learning facilitator, his or her services will still be required.

However, practice must and will change. For many people the 'tell and listen' classroom lecture is the most conventional idea of instruction. It dates back to the medieval period (before the 'reading revolution') when books were in short supply and learned men were given the task of reading extracts to their students. To quote again from the *How do People Learn?* Research Report[2] 'On Classroom Instruction' (p.9), 'While nothing has replaced it yet, especially in terms of cost-efficiency, the model does suffer from some fundamental deficiencies.' As all trainers will recognise, those deficiencies will include: information flows in one direction; experiences can be theoretical with few opportunities for practice; and topics may be disconnected from actual challenges at work. Most important of all, learning is a continuous process whereas classroom instruction takes place during specific times.

In practice, all trainers have developed approaches and techniques which can to some degree compensate for these deficiencies in delivery in the classroom. Moreover, good instruction is emerging as an essential component of any approach to the delivery of training. A particularly interesting insight on the place of instruction to support e-learning has been made by Dr Michelle Selinger of the Cisco Network Academy.[3] Her work is summarised in the case study below.

CASE STUDY

The Cisco Network Academy program

The Cisco Network Academy program is a public-private partnership between the IT company Cisco, governments and educational institutes, which teaches students how to design, build and maintain computer networks. It is taught in 149 countries worldwide with 10,000 other academies, nearly 30,000 students enrolled and over 123,000 graduates (as of December 2002).

Cisco Academy Training Centres (CATCs) train instructors at regional academies, which in turn recruit, train and support up to ten local academies; the local academies teach the students. The e-learning curriculum developed in the USA involves web-based media-rich content, on-line testing and student performance training. It can therefore be regarded as a blended learning programme (see Chapter 5) developed in a whole variety of different contexts across the world.

In 2002 a detailed study was undertaken to investigate learning and teaching practices. Data was gathered using a web-based questionnaire and interviews with 300 students and 100 instructors involving 57 academies in 11 countries in Europe, the Middle East and Africa. Most interestingly, pedagogical practices were examined in each of the countries visited, and their subsequent impact on how the curriculum was taught was assessed.

The findings offer a wealth of information on how culture and context can affect learning and teaching.

The main conclusion offered good news to those of us who are involved in training delivery. The instructors made the program culturally and pedagogically relevant for their students. They were the ones who assisted the students in their preparation for work in their own country by ensuring that the program related to their country's infrastructure and standards. They also made any adaptations to the presentation of the curriculum to ensure that the approach taken fitted the usual learning environment.

To quote from Dr Michelle Selinger, the Cisco Systems education specialist who undertook the study: 'Instructors should be fully aware that they are the most important element to the success of the program.'

My thanks to Michelle Selinger for her assistance with the preparation of this case study.

Getting the most out of instruction brings us back to the discussion on blended learning which was considered in Chapter 5. There is a rich range of approaches available both to deliver training and to stimulate learning. The 'both' is important. As was argued in that section, if we are serious about the term 'blended learning', we must consider learning as well as training.

Dr Peter Honey (the Honey of Honey and Mumford Learning Styles) has written and researched extensively in this area. Table 9 and the two lists below it reproduce some of the material, developed with Dr Bill Lucas, which he presented at a seminar organised run by NHSU (the new corporate university for the NHS). In this analysis he distinguishes between learning modes and learning methods. A mode is a *manner* of doing something; whereas a method is a *way* of doing something. 'Distance learning' is a mode, whereas 'role play' is a method. 'Learning by doing' is a mode, whereas 'coaching' is a method. Methods should be matched to learning objectives.

Table 9 / Modes and methods of learning

Modes (a manner of learning)	Methods (a way of learning)	
Accredited/assessed learning	Acting-up	Peer tutoring
Audit	Action learning sets	Performance review
Book-based	Attachments	Personal development plans
Classroom-based learning	Audio-tape	Placements
Collaborative learning	Audio-visual	Presenting
Computer support systems	Budgeting	Problem-solving
Conferences	Case study	Professional conversations
Courses	Chairing meetings	Projects
Diagnosis	Coaching	Questioning
Distance learning	Clinical meetings	Reading
Distributed learning	Critical incident	Reflecting
e-learning	Delegated tasks	Reporting back
Embedded	Dialogue/debate	Reviewing papers
Employee development schemes	Diaries	Role play
Episodic	Discussion with colleagues	Sabbaticals
Evidence-based practice	Drama	Scenario-planning
Exhibitions	e-mail discussion groups	Secondments
Family learning	Formative assessment	Simulations
Informal learning	Games	Study guides
Inspiration	Giving and receiving feedback	Teaching
Interactive learning	Imitation	Telemedicine and
Knowledge management	Inspection visits	telementoring
Learning by doing (doing by	Instruction	Toolkits
learning)	Job shadowing	Videos
Learning from colleagues	Job rotation	Visits
Learning through libraries/	Job swaps	Writing
learning centres	Joint ward rounds and clinics	
On-line learning	Knowledge sharing	
Open learning	Leading a team	
Opportunistic learning	Learning from mistakes	
Patient-based learning	Learning from role models	
Portfolio-based learning	Learning reviews	
Quality assessment schemes	Lectures	
Residential	Mass media	
Team-based learning	Meetings	
Telephone conferences	Mentoring	
Trial and error	Networking	
Uninterrupted learning	Objective-/target-setting	
Video conferencing	Observation	
Work-based learning	Outdoor pursuits	
	Peer review	

This list was developed by Dr Bill Lucas (see Power Up Your Mind: Learn faster, work smarter*) for NHSU and categorised by Dr Peter Honey.*

FACTORS AFFECTING THE CHOICE OF A LEARNING METHOD

Many factors are likely to affect the choice of method, among them being (in no order of importance):

- the learning objectives
- the number of learners
- the geographical dispersion of learners
- the available time
- the content/subject area
- the facilities/resources (including finance)
- the trainer's competency in use of the chosen method
- the learner's readiness/motivation to learn
- the learner's learning style preferences
- the estimated acceptability of the chosen method (ie that it isn't at variance with values or cultural norms)
- the expected cost return for the method
- the nature of the support/reinforcement to move the learner from superficial to usable knowledge
- the need for flexibility (ie the ability to change direction if feedback indicates a change of method is necessary)
- the assessment requirements.

This list draws on thinking by Dr Peter Honey and Dr Bill Lucas.

Summary

Learning methods: general principles

There are a number of general guidelines that arise from the literature – but they are *very* general.

1 Learning methods should be chosen based on the type of learning objective. The objective – that is to say, the learning outcome – must be clear. The more specific this can be, the more helpful it is when choosing appropriate learning method(s).

2 The content needs to be broken down into small components and each component needs an objective.

3 The more complex the skill to be mastered, the more the learning method(s) needs to be active (as opposed to passive).

4 The deeper the learning requirement, the more the method needs to allow for understanding and internalisation.

5   Do not assume that any one learning method can completely achieve a learning objective. Use a combination of overlapping methods to provide incremental benefit.

6   When choosing learning methods, it is safer to assume non-cooperation from the learner(s).

7   If a passive and active learning method have the same cost, it would always be optimal to choose the more active method. Active methods are more time-consuming than passive methods in addressing a given learning objective, but the higher quality of learning outcome must be balanced against the higher time cost.

8   Keep it simple – use the most straightforward 'minimalist' method(s) to achieve the learning objective.

9   Choose a learning method that is not only likely to achieve the learning objective, but also lends itself to the integrated assessment of progress towards that objective.

This list is based on work undertaken by Dr Peter Honey and Dr Bill Lucas for NHSU.

I am most grateful to NHSU for permission to reproduce these materials.[4]

How, using this analysis, should we regard e-learning? At first glance e-learning could be considered to be a mode, but as was argued in Chapter 5, it creates possibilities that were not previously possible. Action learning offers a good example. This was a term introduced, developed and popularised by Professor Reg Revans. To quote from the definition used by the commentator Andrzej Huczynski (Huczynski, 2001[5]; p.50):

> *It involves groups of managers coming together regularly to work on real-life organisational problems. They form a group which is assisted by a 'set adviser' who acts as a facilitator or resource person to each group.*

The assumption here is that the process of discovery is more important than content and that groups in organisations, by showing expertise, can find their own solution to problems. Although action learning seeks to develop the individual manager, it uses organisational problems as the vehicle for the learning. Action learning follows a number of principles: the person best qualified to solve any problem is the person who has it; the best opportunities to develop managers occur in their own organisations; a self-help approach based on groups can encourage the solution of problems. 'Most importantly, action learning is concerned with *taking actions,* not merely *making recommendations* for actions' (*ibid.*).

What is exciting and new is the way that e-learning, especially the collaborative activity of supported on-line learning (see Chapter 4, p.50 and Chapter 5, pp.64–65), can bring a whole new dimension to action learning. This approach is currently in place at Shell Open University and is described by them in the case study below.

CASE STUDY

Shell Open University

The Shell Open University is implementing a learning strategy in the Shell Group of moving learning out into the business; training centres and training departments are becoming less important, as are formal courses. The key element of the strategy is the adoption of 'workplace learning' for people both 'learning for today' and 'developing for tomorrow'.

The foundation for this is the reusable 'learning nugget' (content), developed by in-house subject matter experts, which can be moved around digitally from within the electronic learning delivery platform database into appropriate learning or coaching events. The learning nuggets are continuously created, refreshed and reused as a result of their application to the learning process

Learning for today is real-time, collaborative, task-based learning on-the-job, supported with a coach/facilitator (in the business – sometimes virtual) using appropriate reusable learning nuggets, designed using blended learning techniques and delivered according to the needs of the business.

Developing for tomorrow is learning from structured 'curriculum-based' programmes delivered locally or regionally but with workshop events designed to similarly apply task-based learning on-the-job, delivered to reflect the planned future needs of staff and the business.

Learning within Shell is becoming an ongoing experience for people. It is being driven by the ability of the Shell Open University to respond to an immediate workplace learning need, be involved in identifying the future skills requirements for the business, anticipate the resulting learning needs and meet the career aspirations of its people.

My thanks to Peter Bentley and Gerry Nicholson of Shell Open University for their assistance with the preparation of this case study.

Encouraging and supporting learning

This section reviews some of the issues involved in encouraging and supporting the learner. Much of what is considered is well developed in the learning and training literature. It is simply a question of reconsidering and reassessing what is known.

One question should be considered at the outset. It could be argued, in some senses, that all individual learning, irrespective of content, is a good thing. This is more of a statement of an ethical standpoint than a precept for action in the organisation. Given this, should the organisation simply create ample learning opportunities and let the individual learners take advantage of them in any way they wish?

There are three reasons why this is not a sensible policy.

First, it is not practicable because often the organisation needs employees to learn something. It is a requirement of their job. Health and safety is always a good example: certain knowledge (and sometimes skills) must be acquired if people are to work in certain sites. Compliance training in the financial services is another.

Dr Peter Honey has addressed the issue of the volunteer learner. In an article written in 2002[6] he recognised that more organisations are both emphasising learning as competitive advantage and encouraging people to take more responsibility for their own learning.

> *But there is often a strange tension between the two. On the one hand, the organisation is acknowledging that its continued success is dependent on people's learning. On the other, it seems to be saying 'It's up to you.'*

> *Surely, if an organisation is really convinced that learning is a priority for its survival, it would realise the folly of leaving something so critical to the whims of individuals. Yet this is exactly the risk many organisations take when they fail to find ways to make learning a requirement.*

He argued that on occasion compulsion is essential.

> *Everyone accepts that, like it or not, these things have to be done the way the organisation wants them to be done. Why should learning be an exception?*

The second reason why an organisation should not simply 'leave it all to the learner' concerns resources. All learning interventions (or certainly all appropriate interventions) may be helpful, but they all absorb resources. Two sorts of resources are spent when employees learn: time and money. There may be the odd exception: individuals can learn in their own rather than the employer's time (on a distance learning MBA course, for example); learning through experience does not involve direct cash expenditure. However, generally resources spent on learning will compete for resources spent on other organisational objectives – some of which have a more immediate evident connection with bottom-line results.

The third reason is that simply making the opportunities available will not produce results. The participation in the offer will depend on individual motivation (it will be the committed volunteer who takes advantage). Many learners, whatever their predisposition towards the opportunity to learn, will require assistance and support in the process. (If we learned nothing else from the early failures of e-learning, we learned that much!) As Peter Honey puts it in the same article, one of the reasons why learning is considered an exception is a widespread belief that learning is something you can't get people to do unless they want to. Here is the link with motivation. However, Peter Honey argues:[6]

> *You can quickly spot the fallacy in this assumption by recalling the many things that you didn't really want to do but, having been made to, you ended up wanting to continue.*

His conclusion is practical.

> *If you want people to share their learning, engage in CPD [continuous personal development], or to spend time e-learning, work out how to make it a non-negotiable requirement. Then bend over backwards to make learning a rewarding experience that people will come to cherish.*

This last point is indeed a powerful one. There are steps that an organisation can and should take to make learning a positive experience. There are also steps that can be taken to support the learner. Some were discussed in the previous chapter, where the learner-centred initiatives were considered and the role of the supportive line manager outlined. Throughout this book, the importance of coaching has been stressed. It is essential that line managers have coaching skills if effective individual and team learning is to be developed. The UK consultant Janice Caplan, in a recent book,[7] talks therefore of coaching as a management style. A summary of her analysis is reproduced below.

Summary

Coaching as a management style

A coaching style of management is one where the managers use coaching techniques in their discussions and dealings with staff. Through these techniques a manager encourages the employees to identify options and seek their own solutions to problems. This style is in direct contrast to a directive one where the manager has the answer and tells the employee how it should be done. ... Another aspect of a coaching style occurs when a manager works with an employee on a more formal coaching basis, perhaps to help that person develop his or her knowledge, acquire a new skill or responsibility. The overall style therefore encompasses both a general approach and a more formal use of techniques.

A coaching style of management is not about 'being the boss', giving directions and instructions and telling people what to do, how they should do it, should have done it, or jumping in with the answer. Rather, a leader's role today is to enable, encourage and facilitate so that staff have a stronger sense of control over their own work and their own time, and so that they identify their own options and solutions to problems. To achieve this the manager also needs to act as a role model of the desired behaviours. Nonetheless, there may be times when the manager will still need to be more directive with a member of staff.

There are many reasons for coaching. These can broadly be grouped into two: coaching in spontaneous circumstances, and coaching to enhance learning and development.

The aim should be for coaching to be part of how managers and staff do things on a normal, day-to-day basis. With coaching they have an opportunity to improve the way they manage, develop their staff, plan for succession, and share knowledge and expertise. For example, they may need to help someone inexperienced to develop a new skill or to take on a new responsibility; they may need to coach a poor performer to help that person reach the desired standard; they may need to find time to help someone sort out a problem or to help people broaden their skills and knowledge to prepare them for promotion.

My thanks to Janice Caplan for permission to reproduce her work.

Generally, as far as the commitment and competence of the line manager is concerned, the latest CIPD survey contains some positive news. This is summarised below.

Summary

The role of the line managers

Findings from the CIPD 2003 Training and Development Survey[8]

Several areas of the 2003 Survey offer insights on the perception and activities of line managers against this enhanced role.

The first group of findings concerns commitment. Here the news is good. When asked how seriously line managers regarded training and development, 35 per cent of respondents reported 'very seriously' and 55 per cent 'seriously'. Less than a tenth of line managers regarded training 'not very seriously' or 'not seriously at all'. (The latter option attracted minuscule support.) True, 41 per cent of respondents agreed that 'lack of manager support' was a major barrier to effective learning in the organisation, but over 57 per cent disagreed. Looking at another question; over three-quarters of correspondents agreed that, over the last five years, training has been taken more seriously by line managers. Incidentally, the results were even more positive for senior managers.

The second group of findings concerned what line managers do and how they do it.

Survey respondents indicated that pre-programme briefing sessions for learners were widely but not universally accepted. (22 per cent of respondents reported that such briefings were used for 'all sessions' and 30 per cent reported that they were used for 'a majority'.) So too are debriefing sessions between line managers and employees when the latter return to work after training (20 per cent respondents reported 'all session'; 31 per cent a majority). There is also widespread use reported of the learner preparing, and the line manager guaranteeing, support for a written statement of action. Practice here is far from perfect: only 12 per cent of respondents reported that line managers are always sufficiently involved in the follow-up to training programmes. Further, 37 per cent of the respondents chose the option that line mangers could be 'slightly more involved' as opposed to 'a lot more involved', which was chosen by 47 per cent. Not only are line managers seen to be committed, but they are also seen to have the ability and knowledge to provide effective support for learning. 26 per cent of respondents reported that line managers in general had a 'great deal of ability' and 60 per cent 'some ability'.

Those, and other responses, are consistent with problem line managers being seen as no more than a recalcitrant rump – or as a feature of a handful of organisations which are indifferent or hostile to training.

The organisation can take all the appropriate steps. However, at the end of the day effective learning must depend on the learner. Which brings us to the subject of motivation, which stalks modern human resource development like the undead in a horror movie. We know it's there and it matters, but we don't really understand how to deal with it.

Motivation is important. As *How Do People Learn?* puts it (p.34):

> *The disposition and commitment of the learner – their motivation to learn – is one of the most critical factors influencing learning effectiveness. Under the right conditions, a strong disposition to learn, enhanced by solid experience and a positive attitude, can lead to exceptional performance.*

Yet, as the report went on, it is difficult to be certain about cause and effect. Indeed other than the fact that we recognise it as essential, we know precious little. More traditional approaches divide motivation into extrinsic factors and intrinsic factors, and the latter seem to be more relevant to the motivation to learn. To quote from the same source (p.34), these factors:

> *stem from inner or self-driven pressures to grow and achieve, and thus include personal desires, the need to conform, the quest for esteem and instinctive urges to solve problems and support other people.*

Individual motivation must be exactly that: individual and personal – every parent of a school-age child knows that all too well. However, a consideration of the People and Performance model (see Chapter 1, Figure 1) shows that well-considered actions can have an effect by increasing the overall level of employee commitment. Indeed, it may be that the word *commitment* is to be preferred to the word *motivation*.

Implementing e-learning

Earlier in this book it was suggested that, as far as e-learning is concerned, we are in the first few years of a 25-year change programme. This inevitably makes it difficult to answer the question 'What should I do about e-learning?', but that question cannot be avoided. In this next section we summarise the results of a study, which was conducted by the CIPD in the autumn of 2002 and published as a Change Agenda with the title 'The Learning Curve'.[9]

A number of organisations were invited to participate in a short study, sharing with the CIPD their experiences and views about what makes for effective e-learning. All the organisations had given some thought to their approach to e-learning: all had training managers who had indicated a willingness to contribute to public debate in the interests of sharing to arrive at best practice.

They were asked:

- What is currently on your agenda?
- What are the strategies are you employing?
- What are the problems you have encountered?
- How are you seeking to overcome them?
- How would you advise others who might be thinking of implementing e-learning?

The ten organisations that participated in the study were varied. They included the large (Defence Management Training had a potential learner base of over 400,000) and the small (Guidant, with just 60 employees in the UK and 1,700 in Europe). They ranged from multinational organisations (Interbrew, Shell and Nestlé) to those that focused entirely on local services (Surrey County Council and Glasgow City Council Housing Services). Given their differences, it would have been surprising if they were all at the same stage and using similar strategies for e-learning.

Generally, progress in e-learning in corporate organisations was best described as tentative and exploratory. Well-considered initiatives were taking place and organisations were asking 'What works?' Although this may be unpalatable to those seeking a quick fix, to make e-learning work every organisation needed to advance up its own learning curve. It may be that pain is inevitable. Reassuringly, it is evident that most organisations saw a clear way forward and were committed to that approach. For all organisations, however, the introduction of e-learning is a demanding change management process.

The main challenges they had faced concerned the following questions:

- If we build it, will they come?
- If they come, will they learn?
- If they learn, does it matter?

The main conclusions from the study were positive and can be summarised as follows:

All the organisations believed that e-learning had an important (and in some cases pivotal) role to play in their future business and learning strategies. No one was seeking to cut back on their commitment to e-learning, still less withdraw. Many could demonstrate considerable resource savings that had arisen from the introduction of e-learning.

The organisations varied tremendously in their strategy for learning, their pace of change, and their desire to be ahead of the field. Each had defined an approach based on a vision of where they wanted to be and how they could utilise technology to help meet their goals. Some wanted to be radically ahead, while some wanted to temper enthusiasm with the benefit of lessons gained from others.

To re-emphasise, every organisation must advance up its own learning curve in what is essentially a change management process. Recognition of the potential is balanced by reflection on what is needed by the individual organisation, and what can be prioritised and achieved within the many business constraints that accompany sound business practice.

Motivation was seen as crucial for effective learning. Support can enhance this tremendously. There is lots of scope here to develop the workplace as an appropriate and supportive environment for learning as well as for working. Line managers play a decisive role in fostering learning, and they in turn deserve support as they undertake a task for which they may get little acknowledgement. Enhanced support and recognition for line managers as learners might be the next step for many organisations.

While there is no universal blueprint, organisations stand a much better chance of making e-learning work if they approach the change management process in a systematic fashion. Hard questions must be asked and appropriate steps taken in each of the following areas: strategic intent, introducing the system, blended learning, content, supporting learning, and measurement and monitoring. It seems hard to see how anyone could make e-learning a success if any of these critical areas are neglected. A summary of some of the findings (extracted from the report) in each of these six areas is set out below.

Summary

Strategic intent

Efficiency, standardisation and value for money are sought by some of the organisations participating in our study when embarking on a strategy for e-learning. They recognise that new technologies offer a means of transforming their approach to the delivery of training. Other organisations have less sweeping ambitions and adopt strategies based around particular issues. These organisations have not embraced such a wide-ranging approach, but have adopted an iterative development-based method around initial test projects.

Introducing the system

The proportion of staff that have access to personal computers at work varies from virtually 100 per cent in some responding organisations, to 50 per cent and 33 per cent in the two local authorities covered by our survey. Access to corporate intranets closely reflects these figures. These proportions are seen as a critical consideration in the development of an e-learning training programme.

Organisations differ in the extent to which they seek a high profile for the introduction of their e-learning initiative. Some respondents argued that successful initiatives 'spoke for themselves' and this was a better approach than a high-risk launch that ran the risk of rebounding.

Blended learning

There is confusion about the meaning of this term. Some participants in the study interpret it as simply combining learning technology with face-to-face transmission, while others emphasise the range of ways that e-learning can be delivered when combined with multiple routes that support and facilitate learning.

Opinions also vary on the usefulness and spread of the concept. Most are convinced that little new has emerged. Some organisations take it as given that training programmes consist of a number of approaches, and have assimilated e-learning alongside conventional training methods. Other organisations see it very much as either/or, preferring to migrate to e-learning wherever possible, while recognising that for some topics, face-to-face training remains the best and most appropriate option.

Content

The limitation of generic content – purchased as suites of materials from major suppliers – came in for repeated criticism, particularly those which addressed interpersonal and management skills. There were, though, fewer negative perceptions with material designed to foster IT skills.

Differences in culture between the UK public and private sector can also become an issue when generic on-line material is used. The quality of generic material is variable, and extreme measures are sometimes necessary when it becomes apparent that learners react negatively.

However, the production of customised web-based modules is a major area of current activity in e-learning. Some organisations have developed content in-house using authoring tools which are part of their e-learning infrastructure. Others have outsourced these activities, using external software houses to produce material to a pre-specified design.

Supporting learning

When asked about the factors that have greatest influence on e-learning effectiveness, overwhelmingly respondents mentioned motivation to learn, and appropriate support. Time to learn was ranked third. Motivation often rests on the extent to which content is seen as relevant, culture-sensitive and reflective of varying learning styles.

Time is an issue of importance for every organisation, with pressures to perform work-related tasks often taking precedence over the need to learn. Protected learning time is sometimes guaranteed, although problematic to implement.

Measurement and monitoring

The emergence of e-learning has thrown the problem of measuring learning into focus as managers grapple with the question of effectiveness and bottom-line impact. Respondents were asked, 'What proportion of total training time (ie time spent by staff learning) would you say was provided through e-learning?' Most had problems answering this question, though some were able to provide an estimate – in one organisation the figures varied across divisions from 65 per cent to 2 per cent. Almost all organisations identified IT as the category with the highest proportion of total training delivered by e-learning.

Current measurement practice concentrates on what employees have accessed and how much time they have spent on-line. Other evaluation practice follows the traditional model – with all its recognised deficiencies.

In the course of the study a set of statements were produced. They represent received wisdom on the steps to be taken in implementing e-learning and are reproduced in the text box below.

RECEIVED WISDOM ON E-LEARNING

- E-learning should be regarded as a change initiative; it should not be seen as a way of saving short-term costs.

- E-learning has to be driven by training, not the technology. You need to have faith in your own knowledge as a training expert.

- There is a choice to be made between, on the one hand, introducing e-learning as part of a significant shift in approach to learning and, on the other, proceeding through a controlled pilot project.

- The proportion of staff who regularly use a PC at work is a critical factor to be considered in the design of any e-learning initiative.

- Appropriate strategies must be developed for employees who do not have access or the necessary skills. The European Computer Driving Licence (ECDL) is receiving considerable attention in this context.

- There may be merit in making an open facility for staff (and their families) to access e-learning, but this should be undertaken to demonstrate a commitment to learning rather than as a way of gaining immediate business benefits.

- Blended learning is seen by many as a process in which appropriate e-learning modules are a precursor to a training session in the classroom.

- The purchase of generic off-the-shelf material is most likely to be of value for IT end users or IT specialist applications.

- There is considerable interest in the generation of bespoke or customised material – either in-house through the use of an authoring system or commissioning from a specialist software supplier.

- Bespoke materials are often first created to meet essential business needs (compulsory training); other popular choices for the early use of bespoke material are performance appraisal, standard procedures or induction.

- Learning resource centres are seen as a useful facility – especially where a significant number of employees do not regularly use a personal computer at work.

- If a learning resource centre is intended to serve a population who are not regular users of personal computers, on-site facilitation is essential.

As has been noted, much of this chapter revisits familiar ground for training. All it seeks to offer is an updated perspective. Much the same could be said of demonstrating as opposed to delivering value. This will form the subject of the final chapter.

REFERENCES AND READING

1   DfES (2002) *Transforming the Way We Learn – A Vision for the Future of ICT in Schools.* Sponsored report.

2   REYNOLDS, J., CALEY, L. and MASON, R. (2002) *How Do People Learn?* Research Report produced by Cambridge Programme for Industry for the CIPD.

3   SELINGER, M. (2004) 'Cultural and Pedagogical Implications of a Global e-learning Programme', *Cambridge Journal of Education.* 34(1). Paper delivered at the e-learn 2003 Conference, Edinburgh, Feb. 2004.

4   I am most grateful to Dr Peter Honey and to Bill Lucas for permission to reproduce these materials. See also Peter Honey's website www.peterhoney.com and LUCAS, B. (2001) *Power Up Your Mind: Learn faster, work smarter.* London, Nicholas Brealey.

5   HUCZYNSKI, A. (2001) *Encyclopedia of Development Methods.* Aldershot, Gower.

6   HONEY, Dr P. (2002) 'Tough love on learning', *People Management,* Vol 9, No. 2, May; p.42.

7   CAPLAN, J. (2003) *Coaching for the Future: How smart companies use coaching and mentoring.* London, the CIPD.

8   CIPD Training and Development 2003 Survey. London, the CIPD.

9   CIPD (2003) 'The Learning Curve', Change Agenda. London, the CIPD.

8

Demonstrating value

Residential courses were generally popular at the investment bank. Although it was difficult to get people away from their desks, once they were there they generally seemed to appreciate the event, especially the course dinners. Directors and the most senior managers acted as visiting after-dinner speakers. We were particularly pleased to have secured the attendance of one of the big names in investment banking who was working on a consultancy basis. He was sent a full brief on the nature of the event, turned up on time and looked positive. He began, 'I've never participated in any training in all my years in the industry. I have never missed it, and am not sure what the point of it is, but I am sure we can look forward to an enjoyable evening . . .'

Demonstrating value is different from delivery value. The former is about the perception of the contribution of function; the latter is about how good trainers are in doing their jobs. It is perfectly possible to be a group of outstanding technicians but to be held in little esteem. The performance measures and metrics used to demonstrate value must make sense to others in the organisation if the contribution of the training function is to be appreciated.

The first section in this last chapter will consider some general issues on resource allocation. Subsequently the emerging topic of human capital will be discussed, and this will be followed by a reappraisal of the place and practice of evaluation. This reappraisal should be avoided by trainers of a traditional mindset and a nervous disposition; it many contain suggestions that shock and offend.

Ultimately, for all organisations the provision of a climate in which people can learn is an act of faith. It is a statement about the type of organisation that the board and senior managers would like to create. This chapter will therefore conclude with a brief statement on this wider vision of learning.

Allocating resources

Questions on the management of the resources to be devoted to learning in the organisation are becoming both more important and more complex. The growing importance is a result of the link between effective learning and the achievement of business objectives: this was the subject of the discussion presented in the first chapter of this book. The growing complexity has arisen for two reasons. First, the responsibility for the effective learning effort is far more dispersed within the organisation: more people at all levels are taking decisions on how much resource should be allocated to individual and team learning. The second reason, and this is linked with the first, is that time is now the scarce resource: the hours spent learning rather than the cash cost of training provision is what matters. This proposition was discussed in Chapter 5.

Resource allocation and management of training has traditionally been seen as a two-level process: the allocation of financial resources and the implementation of effective processes to ensure that the training produces the desired return. The former has been seen as part of the business planning process and the latter is treated as evaluation. A great deal has been written about both of these activities – indeed, a whole industry has sprung up on evaluation.

However, the shift to learning creates a new paradigm. It challenges our existing ways of thinking and demands a new mindset from the practitioner. It must be questioned whether this traditional model of resource allocation and management remains relevant. In fact, there is much value in this tradition, but in some important respects it offers a limited perspective. To introduce this discussion, three linked topics will be explored in turn below. All are concerned with the allocation and management of resources in the modern organisation. These are: high-level questions on the value of human resources; lower-level questions on the evaluation of the contribution of training interventions; issues surrounding demonstrating the value from such interventions.

Valuing human resources

The conclusion advanced at the end of the first chapter of this book was that people are indeed the most important asset. More precisely, it was argued that 'committed individuals who understand the organisation's objectives, have the requisite skills and operate in an environment where they have the opportunity to take the appropriate discretionary behaviour, create powerful business advantages which can be very difficult for a competitor to duplicate' are today's key resource. Such assets are valuable, but how are they to be valued? This question has given rise to the new topic of human capital. Given its emerging importance, the CIPD commissioned Professor Harry Scarbrough of the University of Warwick and Juanita Elias of the University of Leicester to undertake a review. The resulting report was published in 2002.[1] Some of the issues that they realised are set out in the inset summary below. Much of the analysis that follows will be drawn from their analysis and arguments.

Summary

Valuing human resources

The growing importance of intangible assets in determining the value of a company has been the subject of much discussion since the second half of the 1990s. As the so-called knowledge company emerged, so it was recognised that there was a growing disparity between market value (essentially the capitalisation as indicated on the stock exchange) and book value (what is expressed in accounts). The value of people is just one aspect of this disparity. Brand, reputation, customer relationships, networks and patents can all be described as intangible assets and all have an effect on market value.

As Scarbrough and Elias put it (p.2):

The increasing importance of such assets poses a major challenge to existing methods of accounting and valuation. The scale of that challenge is reflected in the size of the gap

> *between the value of a company's tangible assets in its balance sheet and its stock market value. This so-called 'market-to-book-ratio' is especially high for knowledge intensive firms and service businesses that are especially reliant on human capital. . . . Thus, for some firms, the tangible assets identified on the balance sheet have come to represent only a fraction of their stock market valuation or their value to other firms. The remainder is attributed to the intangible assets provided by brands, R&D and employees. This growing disparity between market and book values not only reflects the growing importance of intangible assets; it also dramatically exposes the limitations of traditional accounting practices in identifying and measuring the value-adding elements of the firm.*

Perhaps the most stark illustration of the difficulties that can arise in providing a market valuation occurred as the so-called Dotcom boom, which was discussed in Chapter 1. Many of these highly valued companies had no more assets than a group of able, generally young, people who were thought to have an understanding of the Internet and some, often embryonic, business idea designed to take advantage of connectivity.

The evaluation of intangible assets in general, and human capital in particular, will be an ongoing subject of discussion. There is a considerable way to go. At this stage in the debate there is no universally accepted definition of 'human capital'. The OECD definition has gained some acceptance (OECD, 1996[2]):

> *Human capital is defined here as the knowledge that individuals acquire during life and use to produce goods and services or ideas in market or non-market circumstances.*

As can be seen, this definition embraces both capability (the knowledge that individuals acquire) and its application. More generally, views of human capital revolve around a core specification which is to do with employee competencies (sometimes equated with knowledge), together with the application of such competencies (hence the inclusion of motivation or commitment in some definitions).

'Human capital as measurement' is just one aspect of the concept. What was refreshing about the work of Scarbrough and Elias is that they were able to introduce another dimension to the debate. Their contribution developed from a case study analysis of organisations that were investigated and measured human capital from the perspective of the need to manage valued people resources. They argued that (p.58):

> *In analysing the experiences of our case firms, it has become clear that firms arrive at the issue of evaluating human capital from a variety of directions. Some were stimulated by external pressures and others by internal concerns. Despite their diversity, however, there were also some important common features in their experience – an increasing desire for greater understanding of employee knowledge and skills, coupled, in some cases, with the development of competence systems and the use of IT. The pursuit of more detailed information on employees is not, of course, in itself a major change in HR practice. In some instances, the provision of such information was linked primarily to performance and development objectives, building on existing HR practice. In other areas, however, we can discern signs of a wider business and strategic agenda.*

This led them to the following overall conclusion (p.59):

> *In theoretical terms, we can see that the notion of human capital is most usefully viewed as a bridging concept – that is, it spans several different domains of theory and practice. These include the links that it makes between theories of firm performance and models of the management of employees. In terms of practice, moreover, it links HR practices for the development and evaluation of employee competencies to the determination of economic added value.*

A starting point is to ask why organisations wish to measure human capital. A first answer is that the traditional balance sheet records only tangible assets and company accounts record the costs associated with people and not the benefits they bring.

Human capital can be viewed both as something which employees bring to the organisation, and as something that is also developed through training and experience within the organisation. This dual dimension means that measurement is a difficult concept. Two other aspects of human capital make measurement complex. First, human capital is associated with the individual – and leaves the organisation when the individual leaves. Second, human capital is dependent on its context. Acquired knowledge may be of value in some circumstances but impossible to apply in others. This has all led to the received wisdom that it is easier to destroy human capital than create it.

However, individual and team learning must certainly create human capital in organisations – whatever definition is used and whatever perspective is adopted. Indeed, the emergence and recognition of the term 'human capital' can be seen as a reflection of the importance of capable staff who are applying their skills and knowledge. What is encouraging, from the standpoint of the training professional, is the emphasis on the judicious use of competency systems as a potential measurement tool. As was seen in Chapter 6, where 'learner-centred interventions' were considered, this is precisely the focus of current attention for many thoughtful training managers. If appropriate connections can be made, the role of human resources as an asset provider, rather than as a cost of production, can be reinforced. This is an exciting development.

Evaluation

The previous section suggests that, in measuring human capital, we are just embarking on the journey. As far as evaluating training is concerned, surely we have reached journey's end? There is a remarkable consensus that one predominant framework – that developed a quarter of a century ago by Donald Kirkpatrick[3] – is fundamentally correct in its approach and any difficulties surrounded its implementation.

The Kirkpatrick model offers four levels of evaluation:

- reaction – how well did training participants like the programme?
- learning – what knowledge (principles, facts and techniques) did participants gain from the programme?
- behaviour – what positive changes in participants' job behaviour stemmed from the training programme?

- results – what were the training programme's organisational effects in terms of reduced costs, improved quality of work, increase quantity of work, and so forth?

Efforts over the years have gone into producing instruments and questionnaires designed to capture information at the various Kirkpatrick levels. There has been recognition of the problems inherent in isolating the effects of a training intervention against a background of changing business conditions. There has been a whole new literature, much of it developed by the US commentator Jack Phillips on return on investment (ROI). Phillips has developed for ROI, building on Kirkpatrick's four levels, a fifth level which compares the monetary value of the results of a programme with the cost. Under certain circumstances, particularly for large training programmes where there is a large commitment of resources, ROI is an attractive, indeed compelling, concept. The ROI literature is worthy of exploration.[4] A full review of some of the more sophisticated approaches to evaluation has recently been published by the Institute for Employment Studies (IES), an organisation that undertakes research with employment issues.[5]

However, a consensus on evaluation should not necessarily give grounds for complacency. Two important questions should be asked. The first is disarmingly simple: 'If we know what's required, why don't we do it?' The second is even more provocative: 'Does it matter anyway?' One can almost hear the training walls of Jericho come tumbling down! Such questions should not be asked! However, they are questions that demand an answer. They are both, as will be demonstrated, given new complexity and new importance in the shift from training to learning.

Consider current evaluation practice. As the IES Report put it (p.ix):

> *Training evaluation is a bit like eating five portions of fruit a day: everyone knows they are supposed to do it, everyone says that they are planning to do it better in the future, and few people admit to having it right.*

There is consistent evidence that the most frequently used method of training evaluation is the end-of-course questionnaire or 'happy sheet' (as it is often known). Generally, surveys are reporting increased use of written objectives agreed with line managers, but little evidence of widespread high-level evaluation.

To understand the reasons why evaluation may not take place beyond the reaction level, and to link to the second question of whether this matters, it is helpful to present an illustration of good evaluation practice. This took place in an investment bank. This may appear surprising, given the bad press the sector has received in the introductory sections in each chapter. However, there were areas where considered leadership, supportive of training, was applied. Once such was Corporate Finance where a director, Clive Baker (he deserves to be named), was responsible for the introduction of a two-day team leadership module.

This module represented an important departure from previous practice. Most of the team leaders had received little if any training in the softer management areas. There was nothing unusual or especially commendable in what could be described as good practice training. Normally, any further evaluation would be left to the training professional who might undertake further evaluation, which could involve assessment at the higher Kirkpatrick levels.

In the case under consideration, however, the director concerned called all participants together over a sandwich lunch. He pressed them individually on the value of the course to the organisation, the areas in which it could be improved, who else should attend (participants suggested that it should be made compulsory for their bosses, the directors!) and the personal agenda that participants had developed as a result of the event and how they would implement it. The course design was improved, and participants were encouraged to apply what they had learned, and their learning was reinforced.

This is scarcely rocket science. However, it was a good example of what has been called 'evaluation as intervention'.[6] It was effective because it took place. It took place because it mattered to the director concerned: he had taken ownership. Because it mattered, he was prepared to find the (most appropriate) time and he transmitted his commitment to others. This intervention had far more impact than any detailed report prepared by a training professional (however 'thorough' in approach) which no one bothered to read.

Moving on, preparation of higher-level evaluation information (on learning, behaviour and results) is conceptually difficult but not impossible. It is however very time-consuming and time is now a scarce resource. The detailed assembly of information from interviews and other sources, and its analysis, is a resource-intensive activity. Put simply, it will not take place unless it matters and people want and use the results. Instead, efforts will be diverted to more compelling business activities.

Monitoring learning resources

How then should resources be managed in the age of the learner? The first thing to be said is that much learning cannot be measured, and this may be the most valuable kind. The second is that even if it could be measured, such activities may not be worthwhile.

An illustration may assist at this stage. In Chapter 4, the Ernst & Young virtual classroom was outlined. It was a particularly strong example of the collaborative use of e-learning. Professional staff registered to participate in an on-line classroom where the tutor was a subject matter expert from within the organisation. As was noted, this initiative has proved to be a considerable success. It has captured the imagination of senior managers in the organisation. Without any marketing it is likely to grow so that up to ten sessions a month could take place. First-level evaluation data is produced electronically at the end of each session. Should a major evaluation exercise be put in place beyond an examination of this data?

There is a case that it should. Undoubtedly such an exercise would provide useful information on the most effective design of future developments of the virtual classroom (evaluation as intervention). However, such exercises may not be as important for resource allocation as the traditional model would lead us to believe. Time is the scarce resource in Ernst & Young, as it is in every professional services firm. It is the individual's manager in conjunction with the learner who will determine whether time spent in the virtual classroom is well spent. It is this decision that will ration its use.

One other issue has been introduced in the discussion above. This concerns the new quantity of information produced from e-learning. At its simplest this can be described as clickstream data (to borrow a commercial term). When people explore a website, their mouse-click generates information then reflects their behaviour. It the website is an e-learning module, it is relatively easy to generate a whole amount of data and many organisations are doing this. How valuable is such data?

Much of the data is activity data. The starting point is information on how many people visited the site and accessed the learning module, how long they spent on it, and whether they returned. A second category is test data. Pre-module tests and post-module tests can be included and used to assess any learning gain. A third category of data is the post-course evaluation, which asks (at Kirkpatrick level 1) what participants thought of the module.

Each of these three sorts of data has its place. It offers some useful information on what is going on, particularly when collected and analysed on a regular basis over time. It is particularly useful when considering the management of the e-learning initiative itself and monitoring the spread and acceptance of e-learning. It is not, however, with the arguable exception of test data, information on learning.

Overall, a review of the literature on the evaluation of e-learning programmes leaves the reader with an uneasy feeling. There is a mismatch between what is required (tangible information on learning outcomes) and what can be supplied (a lot of data on the activities undertaken by the individual learners). The new technology undoubtedly has the potential to supply information which can shed light on learning – quite how is yet to be determined.

It is evident that much discussion and much work is likely to be needed on the linked topic of metrics and measurement, resource allocation and the evaluation of the interventions. A first step is to shed much of the traditional thinking which has been trainer- rather than learner-centred. Much of the emphasis on evaluation as a set of stages seems to have been designed to justify the role of the training department. Once a different mindset is adopted, new questions can be formulated and new approaches adopted.

Inevitably, a certain amount of politics is involved in all this. Consider the following argument. The information that is assembled must in future be designed to support and manage the shift to learning from training. How this information is prepared, and how it is arrived at, will depend on where the power lies in the organisation. How convinced are those who have the power to facilitate (or more importantly prevent) this shift to learning? What sort of information do they need and in what form should it be presented? These people could be the Chief Executive and the most senior management, but in many organisations the case will have been accepted at this level. It may be Heads of Department, line managers or supervisors who need convincing and/or can make best use of relevant information.

As we move to learning from training, more and more people should be taking ownership of learning interventions. The role of the training professional should change to one of ensuring that appropriate evaluation questions are built into the overall learning process and that these will generate appropriate information that is made available to the right people in the right format. This is yet another challenging and exciting task for the future.

A vision for learning

The discussion in these last three chapters indicates that although much progress is being made, there is a way to go in moving a focus to the learner from aspiration to reality. However, the conclusion is positive and the tone optimistic. Hopefully the book as a whole will have left the reader with the following messages. First, there is an attractive future beckoning; second, there is a demanding (but exciting) journey to be undertaken to get there. Learning is different from training because it belongs to the learner. Table 10 summarises just some of the changes required in terms of traditional and emerging roles for the training professional.

If the premise argued in the first chapter of this book is correct, it is the new business forces that are driving the changes. However, there are some important social and public policy issues at take here. Much of government energies are put into activities that are designed to ensure that disadvantaged individuals are not left behind in what has been described as the digital divide. This has led to initiatives like the creation of organisations such as *learndirect* in England and Wales and *learndirect* Scotland which encourage and facilitate participation through access to e-learning. They deserve to succeed. Many corporate organisations have responded positively, as the Selfridges example cited in the case study below demonstrates.

Table 10 / Traditional and emerging roles

How it used to be	How it may become
Focus on training as a top-down intervention	Focus on individual and team learning as an on-going process
Systematic training model is dominant framework	Development of a new paradigm of a focus on the learner
Main responsibility lies with training department	Main responsibility lies with the individual
Line managers direct individuals towards, and support individuals on, training events	Line managers seek learning opportunities for individuals and play an ongoing coaching role
Cash cost of training provision is the scarce resource	Time devoted to learning is the scarce resource
Training department is reactive	Training department becomes proactive
Evaluation reports are prepared based on Kirkpatrick model	Information on effectiveness is made available to those who encourage and support learning
Training professionals design, deliver and manage events	Training professionals play a variety of roles, undertaking a considerable amount of advisory and consultancy work

Learndirect at Selfridges

Selfridges is one of the best-known retailers in the world. It employs 1,700 staff and some 250 managers at its Oxford Street store (where its head office is co-located) and in Manchester. An additional 1,150 concession staff work in the stores. In February 2002, Selfridges established itself as a Learndirect centre, having reached an appropriate arrangement with the Central London North Learndirect hub. It is one of a small number of such centres based in a company.

As a result, staff employed by Selfridges can access and learn from the full catalogue of web-based material available from Learndirect. Concession staff are also eligible if their employer bears the direct cost of the modular training. It was the comprehensive nature of this catalogue – which covers business, information technology and management content – that led Selfridges to adopt this policy. Kate King, Operational Learning Manager, had experience of e-learning in previous roles in the Health Service. She was confident that web-based modules are an appropriate method of learning under the right circumstances, and can offer a cost-effective solution. She emphasises that they must form a part, but never the totality, of the company's offering to its staff. The wide range of materials available through Learndirect offers a sensible way of proceeding to test acceptance.

Learning via the Learndirect modules had proved to be cost-effective, but it requires considerable commitment from the training department. All learners must go through a thorough induction process and tutors/trainers speak with each learner every two weeks. Supported learning, therefore, is very important to the process, and learners view it as important to completed modules.

Selfridges have taken the view that an aggressive promotion of e-learning material would not be appropriate. Learndirect modules are listed as one option in the brochures that all staff receive, and line managers are encouraged to refer to modules during development reviews. Some 50 individuals have signed up to date and are studying a variety of topics, with IT subjects – especially those associated with spreadsheets – predominating. Once enrolled, learners can learn in a designated learning centre at the store, a PC nearer their place of work (but out of sight of the customers) or at home. They receive support and encouragement from a Selfridges tutor, and the company bears the cost.

Kate King agrees that, to an extent, the initial cohort of participants are self-selecting and different feedback may arise from less committed learners. However, to date the initial feedback is encouraging. The content is good and is seen as relevant.

Accessibility and choice of time to learn is a clear advantage, and e-learning is a cost-effective way of enhancing the training offered. Occasionally some IT problems do occur at the Learndirect server.

Kate King's major criticism concerns the bureaucracy and paperwork involved in initial enrolment and in monitoring subsequent progress. A multiplicity of forms require completion and she is

CASE STUDY continued

particularly critical of the need to print out an electronic form and send two paper copies to the hub. It may be that current Learndirect systems are not designed for centres located in a corporate, as opposed to an institutional, environment.

Although it is early days, Selfridges are generally satisfied with progress to date; e-learning will be extended, but on a planned and phased basis. A bespoke package on till training is currently being produced by one of the IT trainers. Encouragingly, the training team feels that the majority of store employees possess sufficiently good IT skills for access barriers not to present a problem.

My thanks to Kate King for her assistance with the preparation of this case study.

Many individuals, sometimes led and often supported by their employers, have taken steps to ensure that they have access to the basic IT skills to allow them to meet the requirements of an information-rich economy. This explains the considerable success of the European Computer Driving Licence (ECDL), which is discussed in the case study below.[7]

CASE STUDY

The European Computer Driving Licence

Introduction

The European Computer Driving Licence (ECDL) is a qualification that enables people to demonstrate their competence in computer skills. The syllabus covers seven modules: three concern fundamental applications (word-processing, spreadsheets and databases) and two concern more sophisticated uses (presentations and information/communications, which centre on use of the Internet). The sixth and seventh modules are integrative (basic concepts of information and using the computer and managing files).

Success in all seven modules – as evidenced by completion of a test – gives the individual an accredited and recognised qualification, the ECDL.

Since its introduction the ECDL has achieved considerable success. In the summer of 2002 the British Computer Society (BCS), which manages the ECDL in the UK, was able to issue a press release announcing that 500,000 people had now registered for the qualification. The worldwide figure then exceeded 2.5 million. The first candidates were registered in the UK in 1997 so, by any standards, this growth is most impressive.

Background

The qualification was first developed in Finland in 1989 and 1990. The seven-module syllabus was developed there, the qualification spread throughout Europe (the ECDL) and, with a different title (the International Computer Driving Licence, ICDL), in other parts of the world. It has been particularly successful in the Nordic countries, the UK, the Irish Republic and Australia. So far it has not established a similar hold in the USA, and this partly reflects a late agreement on the structure for management and promotion of the ICDL in that country.

The ECDL/ICDL is operated by a foundation established by the Council of Professional Information Societies (CEPIS). This organisation was established in 1997. In individual countries (currently over 60) it is managed by the appropriate information or computer society on a licensed basis. The qualification is accredited within the framework that applies in that country.

In the UK, as has been noted, the figure of 500,000 registrations was achieved in summer 2002. By that stage 200,000 people had completed the seven modules successfully and been awarded a qualification accredited by the QCA (Qualifications and Curriculum Authority). The BCS has accredited some 2,500 test centres that can deliver the examination/assessment. This number is increasing at a rate of 30 to 40 per month. Currently, virtually every Further Education College is included in this list, as are some 800 private providers. Some of these private providers are commercial training companies (often with an IT base), some are in-company – for example, the HSBC banking group, Sainsburys and Unilever operate recognised centres. A major boost to the ECDL was given in March 2002 when the National Health Service announced that it had committed to the qualification as part of its modernisation programme and was establishing 200 centres across the UK.

The BCS has to ensure that the test centres operate appropriately and that the integrity of the qualification is maintained. The approach to teaching and learning is a matter for the organisation and the learner. The syllabus can be taught in the classroom or through learning technology (CBT or the intranet) as distance learning.

Successful factors

Why has the ECDL achieved such significant growth? The answer must be that it has fulfilled a need for a recognised statement of competence in basic IT skills. This statement has achieved credibility for the organisation and acceptability among candidates. For this to happen the syllabus must be appropriate, and capable of delivery in a range of organisational contexts. Most importantly, there must be a demand. How has this arisen?

The BCS offers the following explanation. Many companies have been instituting major change programmes involving IT systems. If staff do not have the requisite base skills such change initiatives will fail, be delayed, be ineffective, or face cost overruns. Moreover, an organisation needs some benchmark or yardstick which indicates that a person has these skills at the start of the programme; where there is no such indication, programmes can be put in place to assist the employee to acquire these skills.

A good example is offered by the programme introduced by Glasgow City Housing Services. They developed a special scheme to assist manual staff who have looked after common areas and facilities in housing estates, mainly in multistorey flat developments. Each site has now been equipped with a personal computer. Plans are in hand to use the corporate intranet as a source of information for relevant procedures; they will be networked and various communication tools installed. Of the 750 employees in this group over 400 are participating in the ECDL programme.

For many participants this presents a major challenge, as they do not have the basic PC skills or awareness. ECDL training was therefore offered to all. There was a considerable demand: numbers increased from 200 to 456 during the training manager's holiday break. The delivery method is to use a module, produced by specialist IT trainers, consisting of paper-based material, supported by CD-ROMs. Most importantly, six temporary IT trainers have been assisting these staff and encouraging them to engage and continue. Much of this training has taken place in a busy workstation area, where members of the public seek assistance and support. While it has been of benefit to have the trainer go to the trainee, there has been a downside concerning the learner's ability to concentrate and focus on the learning.

In the words of Graeme Hamilton, the training manager responsible for the Glasgow programme, participants supported the initiative because 'people realised ECDL gave them a ticket to a type of competence'. Recognition lies in the eyes of the organisation and the individual, and this will determine acceptance and growth.

My thanks to the BCS for their assistance in the preparation of this case study.

In 1998 the then Secretary of State for Education and Employment, David Blunkett, wrote the following introduction to an important Green Paper.[8]

> *Learning is the key to prosperity – for each of us as individuals, as well as for the nation as a whole. Investment in human capital will be the foundation of success in the knowledge-based global economy of the twenty-first century. This is why the Government has put learning at the heart of its ambition.*

Government (and Opposition) support for learning is beyond question. Framing and implementing effective policies is far from easy and a critique of what has been achieved lies outside the scope of this volume. Looking to the future, however, one comment can be ventured. If learners are to take more responsibility, they will become a powerful consumer group. Governments find it hard to resist market power but through ill-judged supply-side initiatives they have the capacity to confuse the market and direct energies into the wrong places. This recognition of the power of markets does not mean that a moral stance is impossible. Many people who earn their living by designing, delivering or managing training demonstrate a passion for learning. They believe that the acquisition of knowledge and skills is about much more than simply meeting a short-term corporate requirement. Greater skills give an individual self-confidence above and beyond their immediate application. People who know they will have the opportunity to acquire new skills feel they can cope with the inevitable changes that arise in the modern economy. Learning is a good thing, and its time has come.

REFERENCES AND READING

1   SCARBROUGH, H. and ELIAS, J. (2002) *Evaluating Human Capital*. London, the CIPD.
2   OECD (1996) *Measuring What People Know: Human capital accounting for the knowledge economy*. Paris, OECD. p.22.
3   KIRKPATRICK, D. L. (1975) *Evaluating Training Programs*. Alexandria, Virginia, ASTD.

4 PHILLIPS, J. J. (2003) *Return on Investment in Training and Performance Improvement Programs.* 2nd edition. Oxford. Butterworth Heinemann.

5 TAMKIN, P., YARNALL, J. and KERRIN, M. (2003) *Kirkpatrick and Beyond: A review of models of training evaluation.* IES Report 392. Brighton, IES.

6 For a discussion of evaluation as intervention see EASTERBY-SMITH, M. (1994) *Evaluation of Management Education, Training and Development,* 2nd edition. Aldershot, Gower.

7 For further information on the European Computer Driving Licence see www.ecdl.com,www.ecdl.co.uk,www.bcs.org

8 HMSO (1998) *The Learning Age: A renaissance for a new Britain.* Cm 3790. London, Stationery Office.

Index